ERRATA

On page 77 of the "Good Night" story, an illustration was inserted incorrectly. The third drawing down, across from the text "Then, a great big circle!", should be:

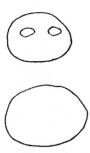

Also, on page 248, the sources for two stories were inadvertently omitted. The text from that page appears below.

Little Boy and Emu
I heard this from a child at a storytelling session in the Alice Springs Public Library. I later found a version in "Thundering Gecko and Emu"by A. C. Van der Leeden (see bibliography). My version is a combination of those two.

The Little Girl and Her Grandmother
This is freely adapted from the collection assembled by Helen T. and Wendell H. Oswalt.

What Can Happen If You Fall into a Hole
Lisa Nell was among a group of children I met at a joint meeting of IBBY and ASSITEJ (International Children's Theater Association), held in Cape Town on September 4, 2004. We shared some drawing stories, and the only one with which I was not familiar was this short one, which Lisa drew for me on a scrap of paper I had in my briefcase.

Drawing Stories from Around the World
and a Sampling of European Handkerchief Stories

Drawing Stories
from Around the World
and a Sampling of European
Handkerchief Stories

Anne Pellowski

LIBRARIES
U N L I M I T E D
A Member of the Greenwood Publishing Group

Westport, Connecticut • London

British Library Cataloguing in Publication Data is available.

Copyright © 2005 by Libraries Unlimited

ISBN: 1-59158-222-9

First published in 2005

Libraries Unlimited, 88 Post Road West, Westport, CT 06881
A Member of the Greenwood Publishing Group, Inc.
www.lu.com

Printed in the United States of America

The paper used in this book complies with the Permanent Paper Standard issued by the National Information Standards Organization (Z39.48–1984).

10 9 8 7 6 5 4 3 2 1

Contents

Acknowledgments

My warmest thanks to Shigeo Watanable, Sachiko Saionji Watanabe, Kiyoko Matsuoka, Tadashi Matsui, and the late Kazue Ishitake, all of Japan. They have been supremely helpful in directing me to many of my drawing stories and giving me good clues so that I could translate the stories into English without distorting them too much. All errors of interpretation are mine.

Grateful thanks are also due to Devon Harle and Robin Youngerman, reference librarians at the Winona Public Library (Minnesota), for their help in getting items for me on interlibrary loans. I had first read many of these items at the New York Public Library. They were rare and often hard to locate, but I needed to check them again firsthand, for the bibliography. What other author has had the delightful moment of hearing on the answering machine, "We have "Hanky Panky" for you at the library"?

I also wish to thank the following, whom I list in alphabetical order, by country:

Mrs. Shpresa Vreto of Albania; the late Jack Davis and the late Ena Noel and all my IBBY friends in Australia; Angela Evdoxiadis and Ruth Brown of Toronto, Canada; Knud-Eigil Hauberg-Tychssen of Denmark; Genevieve Patte of France; the Baumann Family, Barbara Scharioth, Klaus Doderer, and the late Hans Halbey, all of Germany; Bandana Sen of New Delhi, India; Murti Bunanta, Toety Maklis, and Ika Sri Mustika of Indonesia; Nouchine Ansari and all my friends at the Children's Book Council of Iran; the staff at the Folklore Section, Seoul University, Korea; Julinda Abu-Nasr of Lebanon; Ahmed Ghulam Jamaludin, Asmiah Abd. Ghani, Hasniah bt. Husin, Shamsul Khamariah and all my friends at the Dewan Bahasa dan Pustaka, Kuala Lumpur, Malaysia; Joke Thiel-Schoonebeck, Cecile Beijk van Daal, and Rian van de Sande of the Netherlands; Irene Kulman of Paraguay; Sra. Lilly de Cueto of Peru; Kiran Shah, Sheila Wee and members of the Storytelling Group, and members of the Book Development Council, Singapore; Eva Eriksson, Ulla Lundberg, and

Per Gustavsson of Sweden; Susanne Stocklin-Meier and the late Elisabeth Waldmann of Switzerland; Somboon Singkamanen of Thailand; Virginia Betancourt, Carmen Diana Dearden, and many other friends in Venezuela who looked in vain for drawing stories.

In the United States: Ginny Moore Kruse, Kathleen Horning, and Nancy Gloe of Madison, Wisconsin; Cara Olson Kolb and Sam Kolb of Minnesota and California (for their help while with the Peace Corps in Paraguay); Marilyn Iarusso of New York; Nancy D. Munn of Chicago, Illinois; Victor Mair, University of Pennsylvania; and Margaret Read MacDonald of Seattle, Washington.

Abbreviations

IBBY—The International Board on Books for Young People. This is the organization through which I have made many of my best contacts in the field of storytelling. It has national sections in more than sixty countries and has its secretariat in Basel, Switzerland.

USBBY—The U.S. Board on Books for Young People, the official national section of IBBY.

Drawing Stories from Around the World

Introduction

In using the term "drawing stories," I am referring to those stories in which the teller (or an assistant) actually draws a figure or figures while narrating the story. I do not refer to stories in which the figures or pictures are drawn in advance, and the teller then points to them while narrating.

We do not know when drawing stories began. There is some evidence that parts of early cave drawings match commonly known myths and legends in a given area (for example, Australia and southern Africa), but we can only speculate whether the drawings were made during the telling of a tale, or before or after. Most of the sketches in drawing stories from the last 150 years are quite ephemeral, being erased or thrown away shortly after the telling occurs. This makes them very difficult to research.

I first became interested in drawing stories (and indeed, any unusual forms of storytelling) as a librarian and storyteller at the New York Public Library in the late 1950s and early 1960s. This interest was stimulated by Chapter 38 in Laura Ingalls Wilder's book *On the Banks of Plum Creek* and by the appearance of such books as Carl Withers's *The Tale of a Black Cat*. I also saw how the drawing-story books and films of Crockett Johnson (*Harold and the Purple Crayon* and others) had taken hold of the young child's imagination in that same period—and for that matter still do.

During my first extended visit to Japan, in 1972, I came upon a number of children drawing and chanting *ekaki uta*. Thanks to my guide, Sachiko Saionji (now Watanabe), I was introduced to this fascinating aspect of Japanese children's culture. It is difficult to remember now, but she, the late Mitsue Ishitake (founder of the Ohanashi Caravan), or the writer Shigeo Watanabe, sent me the first book in which I

1

saw this custom documented: Satoshi Kako's *Nihon Densho No Asobi Tokumon* (Japanese Traditional Games). Later, Tadashi Matsui, of Fukuinkan Publishers, and Kiyoko Matsuoka, active in the Asian Cultural Center for UNESCO, called my attention to various publications and recordings where *ekaki uta* were to be found. I owe a debt to all of them, because *ekaki uta*, and my first attempts at using them in English, piqued my interest enough to search for drawing stories in other parts of the world.

The drawing storytelling practiced by the Australian Aborigines is surely among the older forms, since it is mentioned by early visitors to the continent. Also, the pictures found in caves reveal that the motifs and sequences depicted show a remarkable similarity to the drawings used in stories told in the past century. Sadly, most folklorists and anthropologists seem to regard this activity as merely a game practiced by children, and only a few of them have given it the serious and careful study it deserves.

The motifs and designs used in such sand storytelling are also used by many serious artists, sometimes using actual sand on bark or other types of paper. They can also be found in drawings and paintings using other art media, such as pen and ink, watercolor, tempera, oil, and the like. The designs have also been used in film. But in virtually all of these cases, little or no mention is made of the use in storytelling.

More scholars have studied the "storyknifing" common among the Napaskiak, Yup'ik, and other groups in Alaska and the area on both sides of the Bering Strait. Storyknifing is generally practiced mostly by children and women. One of the first toys given to children in the past was a beautifully carved bone knife (not sharp) used exclusively for this activity. These storyknives are now collectors' items and carry a hefty price. Nowadays, ordinary table knives of metal or plastic are used.

As soon as the children are old enough to verbalize simple narratives, they draw sequential figures in snow, sand, or mud while telling a tale that matches the pictures. This is the process called storyknifing. According to all the scholars who have studied this activity, the typical commencement for such a session is for one child to suggest to another, "Let's go storyknifing," and they troop out to a space where there is a fresh layer of snow or a nice smooth area of mud or sand. The stories are of the type commonly known as "personal experience" narratives, or they are modeled on traditional folktales known among the children. The tellers often change the details to match their specific life situations. Boys generally drop the activity as soon as they recognize that it is not done by adult men, although there are exceptions.

The Yukaghir are a reindeer-herding people who live in the Yakut area that borders the Arctic Ocean. One of the customs girls carried out during communal dances was to take pieces of fresh birch bark and start carving figures in it with the tip of a sharp knife. The onlookers were made to guess at what the figures represented until all present could arrive at a mutual understanding. The contents invariably related to expressions of love. Only women made these "love letters" as they were called. For many years, certain scholars considered them an early form of writing, but John De Francis, in *Visible Speech*, quite convincingly argues that they were simply mnemonic devices. It is my opinion that this custom is simply another form of "storyknifing" practiced by a people who must at one time or another have been in touch with the Napaskiak, Yup'ik, and similar groups on both sides of the Bering Strait.

It is a curious phenomenon that the art of drawing sequential pictures and telling a story is practiced so similarly among such disparate groups in the South Pacific and the North Pacific.

The Chinese are also early drawing storytellers. There seems to be no firm evidence as to when and how Chinese script was invented, but there are many legends that try to explain its origin. One that is well known goes something like this:

> A long time ago, there was a clever Chinese minister who was walking along one early morning, pondering how he could pass on the words of the Emperor in such a way that even distant subjects would understand. As he walked along, he saw in the ground the prints made by various birds and animals. He realized he could "read" those prints and tell exactly which animal or bird had passed by, and where each was going. If he could invent a way of putting the Emperor's words as sequential marks on some permanent surface, such as bone or bamboo, he would be able to send these words to all parts of China at the same time. He knew the symbols that had been used for centuries on "oracle bones," animal bones that were used to predict future events. He took some of these ancient symbols and combined them with other symbols, each one representing a syllable or whole word. And out of that came the Chinese way of writing.

This is not the place to argue historical proofs for dates when sequential writing began. Suffice it to say, it began very early in Sumeria, in Egypt, and in China, but only in the last-named area does there seem to have developed the custom of telling and drawing stories based on elements of written characters. This may be explained because we only have surviving evidence for the Chinese use of storytelling to elucidate ideograms; there might have been similar storytelling using Egyptian hieroglyphs and Sumerian picture scripts.

Only a small percentage of Chinese characters in use today are true pictographs or ideographs. Most of the characters are phonetic. Nevertheless, there are enough pictures of real persons or objects hidden in the characters, that it is logical for a parent or teacher (who has observed the power of story) to make up a short narrative and tell it while teaching the child, thus making the shape and placement of strokes in the character more memorable.

That this is still the way some Chinese families teach their children characters they want them to remember was brought out very strikingly to me on a visit to the Hillcrest School in Toronto many years ago. There, I met Jasper and Pippin Hitchcock, twin brothers who were Chinese-Canadian. They had been taught an ingenious little story to help them remember the characters of their name as written in Chinese.

When Chinese writing went to Japan, where it became known as *kanji* script, this story-drawing custom obviously went with it. Although Japanese uses its own purely syllabic form of script, the educated person must also learn a certain amount of *kanji*. This was often taught in story form. Masahiro Iwai (1987) points out (p. 82) that *kanji*-writing songs are still known by teachers and by a certain percentage of adults and children in Japan. The same is true in Korea, as shown in *A Korean Night's Entertainment*.

It is not surprising, then, that *ekaki uta*, the picture-drawing story chants, should have developed and flourished and become so widespread among children in Japan today. Most of the scholars who have written about the *ekaki uta* have pointed out that while children in the earlier part of the twentieth century were exposed to no more than forty, now more than one hundred *ekaki uta* are extant among Japanese children. As the main reason for this increase, Iwai cites the lack of play space for present-day Japanese children. Performing *ekaki uta* requires far less space than singing games that demand a lot of body movement in larger, more open space. I personally attribute at least a part of their recent extensive development to the new visuality prevalent in Japanese culture (and in many other parts of the world as well).

The use of Western numbers in so many *ekaki uta* may have stemmed from an entirely different source. It is known that drawing a human head using only the Western numbers from zero to nine was common in Europe as an entertainment. This occurred in many configurations. The custom of drawing a face or head using Japanese numbers and symbols exists from the Edo period, and it was in the latter years of this period that Japan opened to the West. It seems logical to speculate that the two "number" methods of drawing a human head combined and gradually worked their way into the popular forms of entertainment, among them, *ekaki uta*. It is my belief that Japanese children include the Western numbers so frequently in their *ekaki uta* because they are required to learn both systems of writing numbers from early on, and by using them in this manner, they learn them in a memorable way, having fun.

There are similar drawing stories among the languages of India, often relying on the letters of one of their alphabets. I know of them only because of seeing them told by Indians from the various language areas. They are exceedingly difficult to translate and adapt, because they rely on knowledge of alphabets that are used only in specific areas of India. I could find no studies in folklore or anthropology referring to such stories, so I know of no connection with other Asian traditions.

The drawing stories found in the Indonesian and Malaysian areas, on the other hand, all seem to have come from Japanese or Chinese or European traditions. In Indonesia, there are mini-stories created around human head drawings, using Western numbers. These could have been brought in by the Dutch. Ika Sri Mustika of Jakarta and Nusa Tenggara of East Timor both showed me interesting variants.

European drawing stories can be traced back less than two hundred years, and, in most cases, seem to have been popular mostly from the mid-nineteenth century to the early twentieth. The rebus has been a popular device for a much longer period, but it cannot be called a drawing story by my definition, since it usually relies on printed words alternating with pictures that the reader is expected to decipher. However, the popularity of the rebus, especially among newly literate populations, surely helped to foster the acceptance and spread of drawing stories, once they appeared on the scene.

The same is true of the picture sheets used by market singers throughout Europe. The sheets had pictures hand-drawn or printed, and the tellers hung them up and told, or sung, the tale depicted. The common term used for these tellers was *bankelsanger*, or bench singer, because they usually stood on a bench. Two contemporary pictures of such storytellers can be found in my book *The World of Storytelling* (pp. 84–85). Most of these were dramatic stories, culled from the sensational news of the day.

An interesting variant appears in the Kaszubian region of Poland, where the picture sheets were used as a means of keeping alive the Kaszubian language during the period when Prussian authorities were attempting to stamp it out. These sheets were called *Kaszubskie Nuty* and can be seen in the Kaszubian Museum in Kartuzy, Poland. I know of no examples in American museums or libraries. But again, these do not fall within my definition of drawing storytelling, because the drawings were made ahead of time, and the teller/singer simply used a long stick to point at each picture as he performed (they were almost exclusively male performers).

The first mention of a European drawing story I have been able to locate in print is a version of the story often called "The Wild Bird" but titled "The Wolves, the Goats and the Kids" in this collection. It can be found in the Frikell book (1872, p. 89) under the title "Doing a Goose in the Turn of a Hand." The story given with the figure is a scant four lines long, but the general outline is there. The Frikell book was a popular handbook for magicians, both amateur and professional.

The person most likely responsible for the spread of popular, folk drawing stories in Europe was Charles Lutwidge Dodgson, better known as Lewis Carroll, the author of *Alice's Adventures in Wonderland*. He is known to have used them in entertaining children and adults. Or perhaps it was Hans Christian Andersen. Andersen traveled widely throughout Europe and the British Isles. Both he and Carroll were known for their "trick" entertainments. It is possible that one or both shared a drawing story, and this was passed on when they visited various homes. This could account for the fact that similar drawing stories were known in England, the Netherlands, Denmark, and Sweden during the last decades of the nineteenth century. However, it is just as likely that these were pure inventions coming from the common folk and passed quickly from one person to another because they were so clever and quirky.

But how to account for the appearance of these same stories in the United States during the same era? If Laura Ingalls Wilder was correct in her remembrances, her mother was telling her some of these stories some time in the early 1870s. Her memory is backed up by at least two other informants growing up in other parts of the United States at the same time. (See notes at the head of "The Black Cat" and "The Wolves, the Goats and the Kids.")

We shall probably never know exactly where these drawing stories started and how or by whom they were spread. But spread they did, usually by word of mouth and individual drawing, but also in printed picture and text format.

A few of them, such as the one I call "The Smart Shopper" in this collection, seem to be found in all parts of Europe. One can often tell where the variant comes from simply by noting what items are purchased. Others seem to be of more recent vintage and are found only in one area (for example, "Per's Trousers").

It is curious that those immigrants from Europe who went to South and Central America in the nineteenth century did not seem to take the drawing story with them. With the help of many friends and colleagues in various countries of that region, I have searched for drawing stories, but in vain. Perhaps they did take some drawing stories with them, but most did not survive because the contexts of the stories were so different from the daily life around them. In the end, I found only one traditional drawing story, from Paraguay, given in this collection as "How to Get Rid of Mosquitos."

There have been a number of drawing story books used by teachers and librarians for decades (Margaret Oldfield's books come to mind). I have observed some of these stories used skillfully and successfully in storytelling programs for young children. I find it curious, however, that I have never come across the stories from these books repeated and passed on by adults or children in what might be called a folk storytelling situation. Is there something particular about the ones that have survived through live oral and pictorial telling?

One answer might be that the book stories are more generic and seem to be set in no specific place or time. But most of those passed on orally (albeit sometimes kept alive by being recalled through a printed version) seem to be quite specific in their setting and often give an idea of a very definite time when the story took place. If they spread from place to place to place, as, for example, the cat story that begins the collection, they pick up just enough variation to give the story a totally local flavor.

This is the main reason why I personally like to tell these drawing stories, picked up from many sources around the world. The cultural clues are often slight or subtle, but they are there in almost every story. They can provide a connection to another cultural group, if only through a few moments of shared delight in the sheer fun of the clever matching of sketch to story.

A Note on Drawing

In each story I have used the correct drawing stroke opposite the text, at the point when one should be saying those words. For example, in the first story, when one is saying, "There was once a boy named Tommy," one should be drawing the large capital "T." When one is saying "Tommy lived in a house with two rooms," one should be adding the two "rooms" onto the T.

It is important to practice the timing in each of these stories. Do not let the drawing get ahead of the words or vice versa. Because of the nature of Chinese characters and the importance of doing them in beautiful calligraphy when possible, I strongly urge practice of the order of the strokes and the use of a brush and ink pad. Best of all, find a skilled Chinese calligrapher to do them for you, if you can.

For Those Who Feel They Cannot Draw

Although these are often called chalk board stories, instead of drawing them on a blackboard, use a large paper flip chart on a standup easel. Photocopy the final figure in each story, blowing it up as large as possible. Trace them on to your large paper on the flip chart, using a very faint pencil that is not visible to the audience. Make a short written list of the order of strokes, and cover each pencil stroke with a broad felt-tipped pen, as you are telling that part of the story. Chances are, no one in your audience will notice that you are tracing rather than doing an original drawing.

THE BLACK CAT

Nineteenth-Century American

This is perhaps the most widely known drawing story in the world, due in part to the fact that Lewis Carroll, the author of *Alice's Adventures in Wonderland*, used it as an entertainment in the nineteenth century. He was copied by many trying to be as clever as he was. But it is likely that it was a folk story Carroll had adapted. *The Journal of American Folklore* reported two versions in 1897. A rhymed version, with a different cat figure and a completely different text, was written in 1897 by Jane H. Holzer, a teacher in Connecticut. The illustrator Paul Zelinsky used that poem to make his picture book *The Maid and the Mouse and the Odd-Shaped House*. The longest version is also in poetry, but in the Friesian language of the Netherlands. Its main characters are two aunts, whose names begin with "T" and "D." The resulting drawing is different from the one given here. It was published in a picture book, *Fan Tryntsjemuoi en Duotsjemuoi* by Jant Visser-Bakker and Anneke Buizer-Visser. A Dutch version of the same book was also published.

There was once a boy named Tommy.

Here's a T for Tommy.

Tommy's best friend was Sally, who lived down the road on a dairy farm. Here's an S for Sally.

Tommy lived in a house with two rooms.

In each room there was a window.

On the corner of each room was a chimney.

In the front of the house was a wee double door.

On both sides of the doorstep there was grass growing.

[At this point, try to cover the cat's head with your non-drawing hand or arm.]

One day, Tommy took an empty pitcher and set off for Sally's house.

"Do you have some cream?" Tommy asked Sally.
"Yes," said Sally. "We keep it in the cellar."
They went down into the cellar,

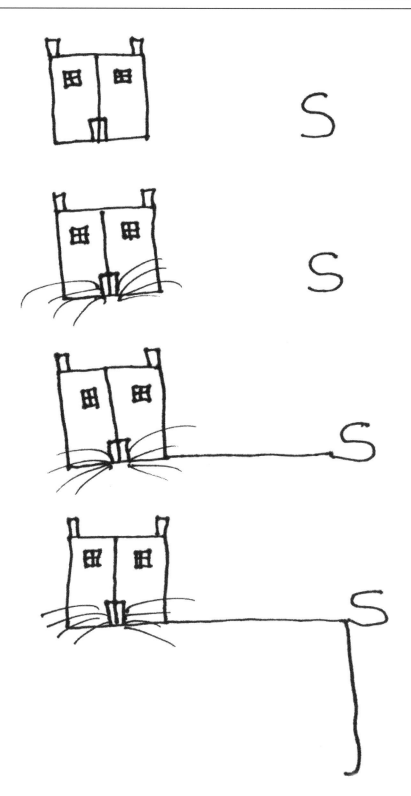

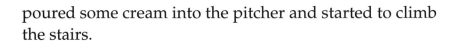

poured some cream into the pitcher and started to climb
the stairs.

Tommy spilled some of the cream on the steps. He and
Sally slipped on it and tumbled back down the steps.

"Let me carry it," said Sally. She took the pitcher. They
climbed up the steps and walked along the short path to
Tommy's house.

Suddenly, Sally spilled some cream from the pitcher. Tommy and Sally went sliding down and then they climbed up.

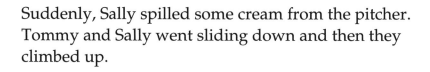

They slid down again and climbed up once more and finally made it back to Tommy's house.

But too bad! There was the black cat waiting and no cream was left in the pitcher. [Lift your hand or arm away from the drawing.]

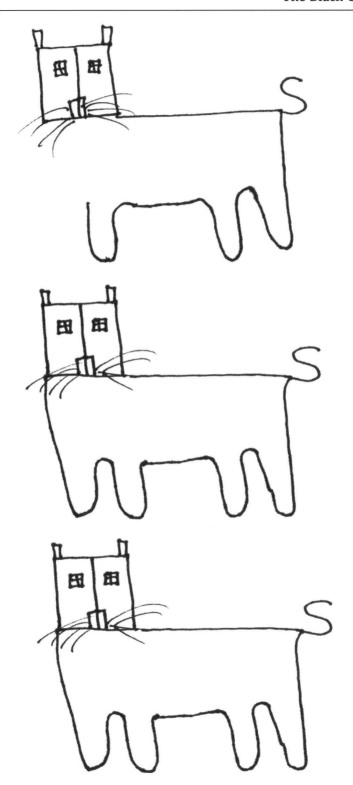

THE WOLVES, THE GOATS
AND THE KIDS

Mongolian

Versions of the picture in this story have been found in Europe, in the United States, in Africa, and in Asia. As mentioned in the Introduction to this section, it seems to be the first European folk drawing story that appeared in print. A version that Laura Ingalls Wilder learned from her mother is featured in "The Day of Games," Chapter 38 of *On the Banks of Plum Creek*. Isak Dinesen, in her book *Out of Africa*, cites another version that she told frequently while living in Africa. It is likely she learned it during her childhood in Denmark. I came upon that version while doing storytelling workshops with a group of librarians and children's book writers in Kenya in 1987. In each case the story that goes with the drawing is different. Here it is set in Mongolia, where rural people still live in round yurts, tents made of thick felt.

If possible, use an erasable chalk or pencil when telling this. Do not worry about making the erasures complete. The marks left behind will later suggest feathers. If you are using a permanent marker, disregard the remarks about erasing.

Once upon a time, in the country of Mongolia, there was an old man and an old woman. Like many people in Mongolia, they lived in a round tent, called a yurt.

In the middle of the tent was a hole to let out the smoke from their fire.

Near their tent was a fenced-in pen where they kept their five black goats and three black kids—the baby goats.

Not far from the pen were two bushes. Hidden behind these bushes, two wolves had their den. If you walked by, you could see only their eyes, shining in the dark shade of the bushes.

One morning, the old man went down to the pen to get the three little black kids. He brought them back to the tent (erase the three small black dots) and tethered them on ropes at the back of the tent, so they could eat the fresh, new grass that was growing there.

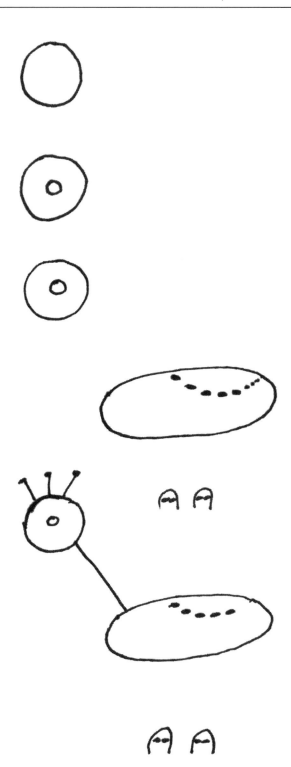

The old man then went outside to have a good look around. When he saw no sign of danger, he went back in the tent to have a glass of tea.

The moment the wolves saw the old man go inside, they ran up to the pen and jumped to the top of the fence.

The five black goats were so frightened at seeing the wolves on the fence, they all jumped over the back gate. [Erase five large dots.] Each goat went in a different direction. They were all bleating and crying.

The old woman heard the commotion. She came out of the tent and ran to the pen. "Oh, where are our goats?" she cried. "I don't see any of them. All I see is a strange bird."

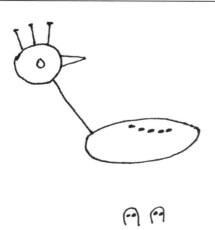

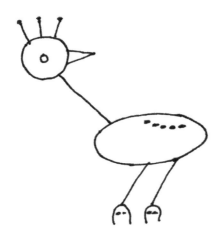

For purposes of introducing other countries, you can do versions of this story as it might be told in rural parts of other countries from around the world. For example, in Masai areas of Kenya, it would be calves penned in, the tents might belong to tourists on safari, and so on.

THE SMART SHOPPER

Romanian, Greek, Armenian

This drawing story has many variations and can be found in all parts of Europe. In most of the versions I have seen, the figure is a woman, and the items she buys are things to eat, and utensils with which to eat. Danish and Swedish versions, as indicated in Per Gustavsson's wonderful book *Ritsagor*, usually draw a child as the shopper. In some places, as in the Swiss version that follows, the figure is drawn right side up, and the shopper pays sixty-six cents for everything. In telling either version, it would be appropriate to put in the name of a local market or convenience store, but be sure to keep the locale of the story in Europe. For example, after "set off for the local market," you could say: "It was a little like _____ in our neighborhood." I recently told this story in Jakarta, Indonesia, and adapted it to fit things bought for a birthday party for one of the children in the day-care center where we were having a demonstration story hour.

One day, a Greek woman went out to shop for food for herself and her husband. She took her shopping bag and set off for the local market.

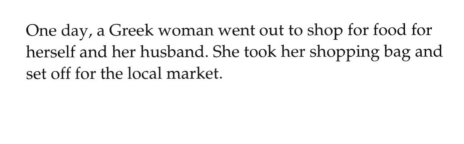

First, she bought a big pumpkin.

Then she bought a smaller melon.

She bought a carrot.

Then she bought four potatoes.

She carefully selected some pea pods and some parsley.

"We need something to eat this with," she said. So she bought two forks.

When she got home she said to her husband, "Aren't I a smart shopper! I got all this for ninety-nine cents!"

[Turn figure right side up.]

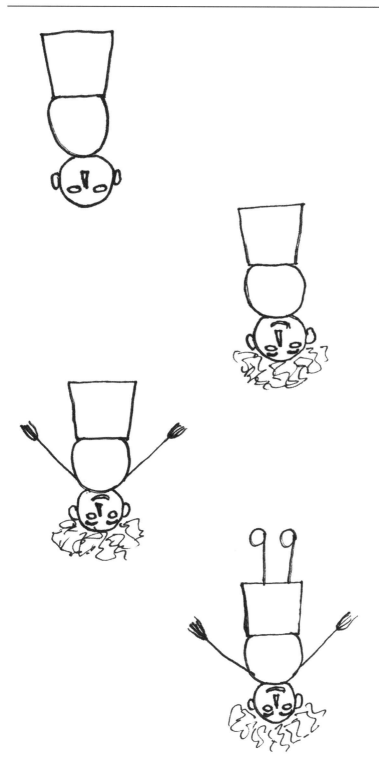

Little children often like to find and name the different objects that make up the figure. You might wish to ask questions such as, What are her eyes made of? Her ears? But don't belabor the process. A fun exercise for almost any age is to have the audience make up their own version of the story, citing things they would buy. A good art exercise to follow this type of drawing story is to show reproductions of some of the paintings of Giuseppe Arcimboldo, Italian artist who lived from 1527 to 1593. He used fruits, vegetables, and flowers to make ingenious portraits. The group can make up their portrait using fruits, vegetables, or flowers. Also, you might wish to use *On Market Street* by Arnold and Anita Lobel (New York: Greenwillow, 1981) in conjunction with these stories.

THE SMART SHOPPER

Swiss Version

In telling this, I like to introduce the German words for Mr. and Mrs.—Herr and Frau. In the blank space where the name of the buyer should go, I usually put the name of a teacher or other person of authority in the audience, especially if it is German-sounding. Little children love to hear the names of their teachers in stories, almost as much as they enjoy hearing their own names.

One day, Frau _____ went to the local store to buy some things. "*Guten Tag,* Good Day, Herr _____," she said to the owner. "I would like to have two eggs, a sausage, and one of those gingerbread hearts."

The grocer put all the things in a bag and tied it up nicely.

"Oh. I almost forgot. I need two breakfast rolls, and a sack of your best flour."

Just as she was going out the door, Frau _____ remembered she needed some mushrooms.

"And you might as well give me two of those forks you have on sale," said Frau _____.

"That's it, then, how much does it come to?"

"All together, it comes to sixty-six cents, Frau _____. *Dankeschon.* Thank you. Come again."

Now wasn't she a smart shopper!

WHAT DO YOU THINK YOU ARE?

German, Swiss

Here is a drawing story that usually requires two participants. It is most often initiated by an older child (the teller) trying to trick a younger child (the drawer). Usually, this younger child has just learned to write the alphabet. It is typical of the kind of story young children like to try on their even younger peers, to see if they will catch on before admitting to something silly or stupid. A commonly known one has the teller asking the listener to repeat "Just like me" after every sentence of the story.

When doing this for an audience of young children, it would be appropriate to tell it as I give it here, rather than attempting to ask one child to be the guinea pig (pun intended!). When telling to kindergarten or first grade, it is fun to have the children, each with a small piece of paper and pencil, draw along with you. They are simply so involved in getting the letters right, they do not see the end coming. I once told this to an audience of three hundred first-graders in a school in Singapore, each of whom was drawing along with me, and they exploded with laughter at the end. They giggled and laughed at the variety of pigs they had made: some fat, some skinny, some looking more like dogs, some looking like no animal at all! It is a perfect way to end a program, and give the children a story to take home and try out on parents or siblings.

There was once a brother and sister who lived on a farm in Germany. One day Gretchen asked her little brother, Hans, "Can you print all the letters of the alphabet now?"

"Oh, yes, I know them all," said Hans.

"Then print your name here," said Gretchen. Hans printed his name in large capital letters.

"Do you know how to make an M, for mother?" she asked.

"Of course," said Hans.

"Then put an M over the H, right there"

"How about W? Can you print that?"

"Sure," said Hans. "Where do you want it?"

"Make two of them, one under the H and one under the S." Hans printed the two W's.

HANS

M
HANS

M
HANS
W   W

"Now put a capital C, right here in front of the H, but not too close." Hans printed the C.

"I think that S is lonely," said his sister. "It needs a small s. Put one just at the top and to the side."

Hans made a smaller s near the big S.

"Can you make small letters as well?" asked Gretchen. "If you can, make a small o right here between the C and the H?"

Hans made a small o.

"Now, connect all the capital letters with lines," said Gretchen. "Connect the C to the M, the M to the S, the S to the W, the W to the W, the W to the C. What do you think you are, Hansi?"

M
C HANS W
W W

M
C HANS S
W W

M
C °HANS S
W W

THE KEY

Danish

A wonderful introduction to any program about castles or princes and princesses, this story is made even more impressive if you can find a large metal key in this shape. Show it only after you have completed the story. Other Danish versions cite a princess as the main character. Choose whichever you prefer.

There was once a Prince who lived in a castle with three towers. Here is his castle.

It was always very busy in the castle. One day, the Prince decided to go for a walk. He walked around to the side of the castle and along the straight path in front of it. After a while he came to a big lake.

He saw that there was an island in the lake.

It wasn't far, so he swam to the island and played there all day, having fun all by himself, with no one to order him about.

Suddenly, he noticed it was beginning to get dark. He started to walk back on the path. But it was so dark he did not see that he was walking slightly above the path. He did not notice the big stone right at the edge.

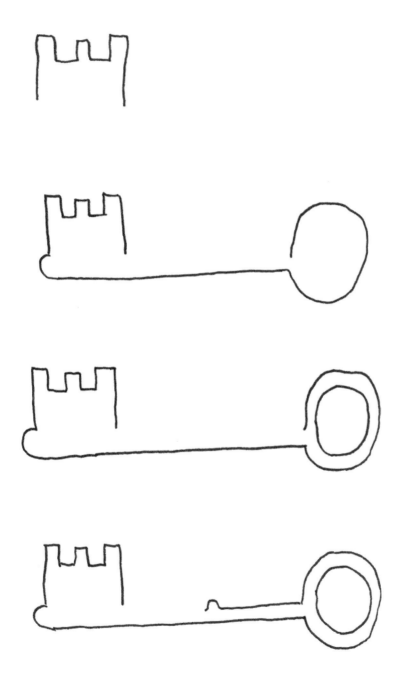

He stumbled, bumped against another stone, and continued on his way.

But before long, he bumped against a third stone, a bigger one.

When he arrived at the castle door, he could not open it because he had lost his key when he stumbled in the dark.

Who can help him find the key?

For picture-book hours, an appropriate book to use in conjunction with this story is *The Key to the Kingdom* by Betsy Maestro (New York: Harcourt Brace, 1982), a picture book based on a very old cumulative rhyme. The story could also be used as an introduction to other locking devices, modern and old. One could explore the times and places where one locks things up and where one does not do so.

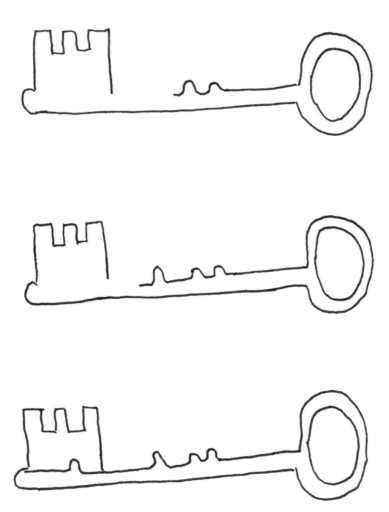

PER'S TROUSERS

Swedish

While drawing stories of this type can be found in many European countries, this one seems to be unique to Sweden. I learned it from Per Gustavsson, one of Sweden's best-known storytellers. He states that it has been known in Sweden since the early 1900s. I use the name Per for the boy in the story, which is pronounced "pear," like the fruit. But if you want to use this story with a very famous Swedish children's book called *Pelle's New Suit* by Elsa Beskow, you might want to substitute the name Pelle.

Per is a Swedish boy. This is where he lives.

His best friend is Lisa. She lives over here.

One day Per went over to Lisa's house and asked her if she would like to go outside and play on a nearby hill.

Lisa said yes, so they went tumbling down the curvy hill.

Then they walked along a short path.

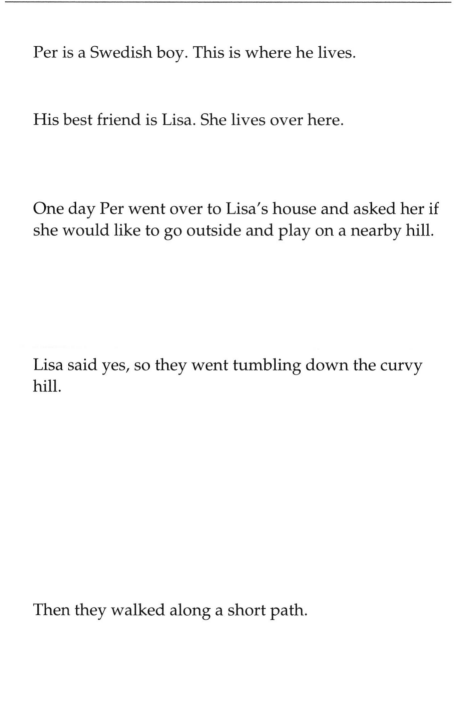

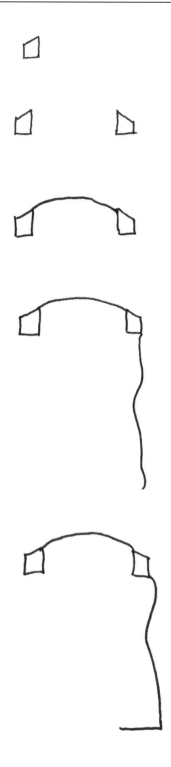

After that, they started climbing back up the hill on a different path.

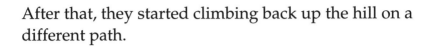

Suddenly, with a swish, they fell back down.

[Make the downward stroke very fast.]

But oh, my! Per had a big tear in his trousers. They had to go home. They walked along another short path.

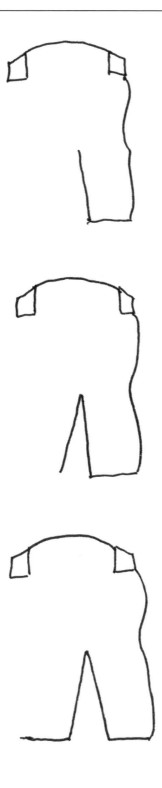

Finally, they climbed the other side of the curvy hill back to his house. No one was at home.

"Let's go to my house," said Lisa. Per followed her home.

Lisa's mother mended Per's trousers. [Shade in space at waist.]

"There you are!" she said. "All fine again."

The name for trousers in Swedish is *byxor*. How many names can you find for "trousers" in English (some examples: pants, slacks, jeans, knickers, etc.). What are some of the slang names? Do you know the names for trousers in another language?

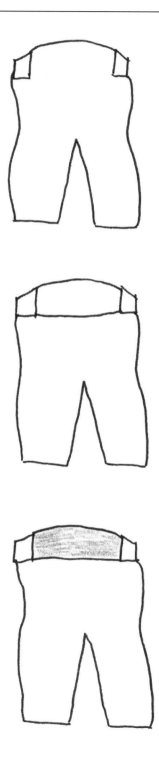

LIGHT BULB

Swedish, American

This is actually only based on a traditional drawing story. The original, which has been around at least since the 1940s, is a slightly vulgar tale about a woman in a girdle and what happens when she bends over. It is curious that it was reported extensively in Sweden in the post–World War II years, but was obviously known in the United States as well. Did soldiers in that war exchange it? We will probably never know.

Katy Horning, of the Cooperative Children's Book Center in Madison, Wisconsin, remembers it well from her school years while growing up in the 1960s in Des Moines, Iowa. I have also found a number of other adults who were teen-agers in those years, who remembered the drawing, but no story.

Here, Nisse is used as the name of a Swedish boy. If you wish to tie this in to a Christmas program, turn him into the Danish Christmas elf, called a *nisse*. You must then explain what a *nisse* is.

Here is Nisse, peeping over the top of something. It is a book, because Nisse likes nothing better than to read. It is his favorite activity.

You can often find him sitting there, head behind his book, reading away, reading away.

However, Nisse also likes music. Sometimes you see him behind his music stand, playing the flute. He loves to tootle away for hours at a time.

Some weeks he reads or plays the flute every day for hours. He forgets to tidy up his room.

Soon, dust balls gather all around the floor of his room.

His Papa scolds him: "Nisse, son, if you do not tidy up this room, I will take away your books and your flute! [For a Christmas version, I usually have the father threaten he will not take *nisse* along to the homes where he leaves treats.]

So Nisse takes the vacuum cleaner and vacuums all around the room.

All of a sudden the room is very dark. "I can't finish vacuuming," says Nisse. "The light bulb has burned out."

"Well, here is another one!" says Papa.

There are not many *nisse* picture books actually showing what a *nisse* looks like, but one that can be found in some libraries is *The Nisse from Timsgaard* by Vilhelm Bersoe (New York: Coward, McCann, 1972). Christmas books that cover Denmark, Norway, and Sweden often have pictures showing the elf as he is known in old Christmas pictures from those countries. In Sweden, he is usually called the Christmas *tomten*. At any rate, the antics of these playful, sometimes naughty, but mostly kind, small creatures are common to much of Nordic folklore. They are somewhat similar to the nixie of British Isles folklore.

HOW TO GET RID OF MOSQUITOS

Paraguayan

I have never encountered this figure in any other country. There are not many bulldogs in Paraguay. Perhaps the story entered Paraguay with the German Mennonites who settled there in large numbers in the nineteenth century.

There was once a mother in Paraguay who had two children. Here are her two children.

One day she took them out to play on the patio behind their house.

Below the patio there was a large *olla*, a pot, in which they kept the water used for watering the plants. It was also a favorite place for mosquitos to lay their eggs.

When the mother noticed a lot of mosquitos flying around her children, she put a mosquito net around one side of the patio.

She put a second mosquito net around the other side of the patio.

But the mosquitos still seemed to be flying around the patio. So she emptied the pot of water. [Shade in the area of pot.]

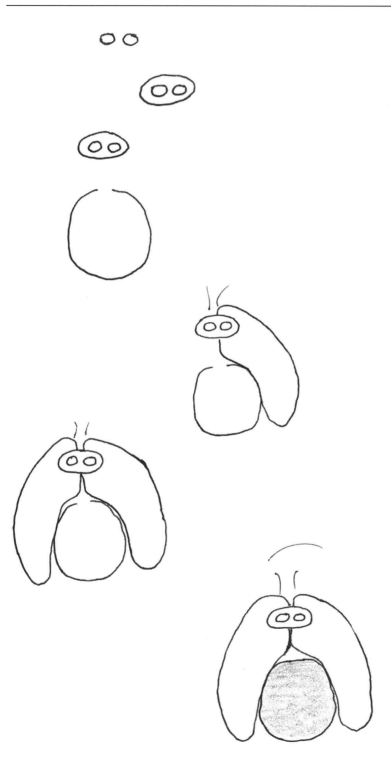

Then she put a huge third mosquito net around everything.

The children did not like being enclosed in all those nets. First one punched a hole in the net. Then the second child punched a hole in the net.

The wind came along and blew the torn netting out above the holes.

When the mother came out again, there were no more mosquitos—only a bulldog guarding her children!

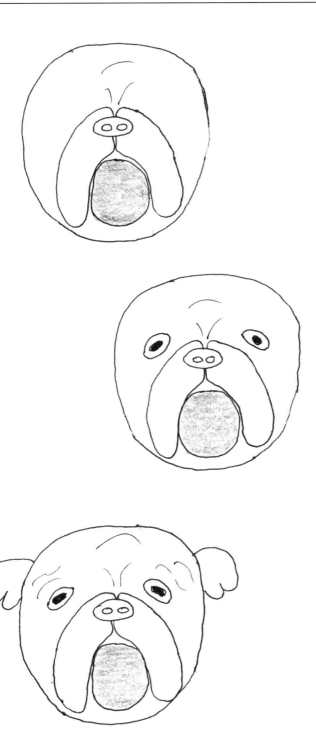

LITTLE CIRCLE, BIG CIRCLE

Indonesian

Virtually all teachers of young children in Indonesia seem to be aware of this charming story. A variant is also known in Malaysia (see the following story). It should really be sung, preferably originally in Bahasa Indonesia and then in English. If you cannot find someone to sing it in Bahasa, at least try to say a few of the phrases. The full text in Bahasa is given in the "Sources" section, together with instructions on how to sing it. The end picture is interpreted differently by children, depending on where they grow up. Some see a teddy bear, others a pig, still others a koala or a monkey. After performing the story, ask the children what they see. Discuss what other animal might be in the picture, depending on who is looking at it. Children of the rain forest seem to perceive only a monkey in the drawing.

Little circle,
Little circle,
Bigger circle.

Little circle,
Little circle,
Big, big circle

Add a banana,
Add a banana

Add a big banana

Little circle,
Little circle

Coiling up and around.

A six, times six;

That makes thirty-six.

A six, a six

Add an angle!
And what do you think is there?

GOOD NIGHT!

Malaysian

This drawing story figure could have originated in Japan, where a similar figure is widely known. In the Indonesian version, as mentioned in the previous tale, this is performed while singing a delightful song. In Malaysia, it is commonly told to small children as a preparation for bedtime or naptime, or during the evenings of Ramadan.

A small circle; a small circle.

Now, a bigger circle.

Then, a great big circle!

Six times six;

That makes thirty-six.

Another six and six;

I love Papa! I love Mama!

Good Night!

And what happens?

A teddy bear appears, to go with you to bed.

RIGHT ANSWER, WRONG ANSWER

Malaysian

It is always interesting to have stories that give two sides of a demonstration or question. Here is a story, in two versions, with which most students can identify. Tell both versions and then ask the audience which they prefer. What does this tell us about at least some children in Malaysia, and their attitude to school? If you can get hold of some Malaysian *ringgit* coins, you can show those in advance and there is no need to explain what *ringgit* are. Otherwise, before telling the story, explain that ten *ringgit* are the approximate equivalent of four dollars.

It rained,
and rained,
and rained,
and rained.

The waves came.

Father gave me ten *ringgit*. Mother gave me ten *ringgit*.

I went to school.

Teacher asked: "How much is three plus three?"

I answered: "Six."

Teacher said: "That is correct!."

So now I can go home.

RIGHT ANSWER, WRONG ANSWER
(Second Version)

Do exactly the same for the first four drawings, up through the phrase: "I went to school." Then change as follows.

Teacher asked me: "How much is three plus three?

I answered: "Three plus three is eight!"

Teacher said: "Wrong!"

"Now you must stay after school."

THE *DOH* BIRD

Bengali

Like many of the Japanese *ekaki uta,* this is full of puns in the original Bengali. For example, to count from one to five in Bengali, one says: *ek, doi, teen, char, panch*. The *doi* or two is written exactly as the figure in the feet is given below. The letter that has the "d" sound in Bengali is pronounced *"doh"* and is written like the first figure in the drawing below (although the tail is somewhat exaggerated here for purposes of the story). Before telling this, I do not explain about *doh* and *doi,* unless I know I have children from India or Bangladesh in the audience. However, after telling it to children eight and older, it is fun to show how we can make up stories using pictures hidden in some of our numbers and letters.

The *Doh* had a bellyache.

A really bad bellyache.

Auntie came along and said: "Here are two stools. Sit down and take a rest."

The bellyache got worse.

Auntie called the doctor. The doctor took a good look all over *Doh*.

He gave him a pill. Now tell me, is he a dodo bird?

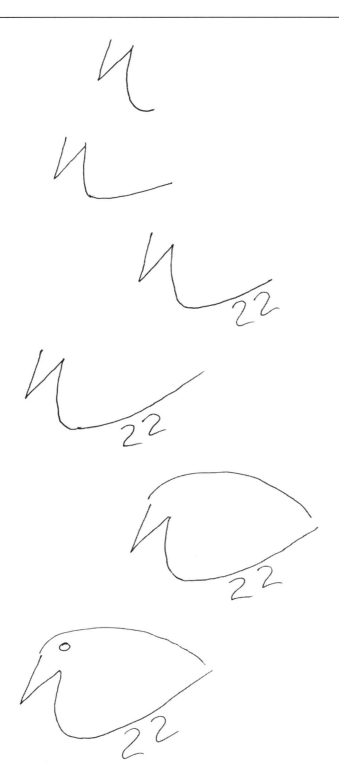

HOW MAN AND WOMAN FOUND
THEIR PLACE IN THE WORLD

Chinese

There are numerous legends that tell how Chinese first came to be written down using strokes that sometimes make a picture. One is given in the introduction. As stated there, some Chinese characters are based on pictures of the words they signify, but most are not. Still, a clever person can usually find a picture hidden in the character. In some Chinese families, short stories are invented to help the children remember key characters that represent names and facts in that family's history.

If you have a friend or relative who knows how to do Chinese calligraphy, invite him or her to draw the characters as you tell the story. The ideographs to the right depict the word or words capitalized in each sentence below. The small letters indicate the order of the strokes and the point at which each stroke begins. In other words, in the first character, for Man, one must begin the second stroke at the top, where the small "b" is located, and not go from bottom to top.

91

Long ago, Man stood up and started to walk on two feet, like this.

Now Man thought he was the center of the universe. He looked around and saw that he was quite small in comparison to many things around him. So Man stretched out his arms to feel Big and Tall.

But wherever Man looked, there was something bigger than he was. Most of all, when he looked up he saw the Heavens above.

Man tried to pierce the heavens. He became a Learned Man and a Worker.

He bought a Field and began to grow rice.

He planted a Tree near his field, so that he would have shade in which to rest after working in the rice field.

But he still lacked something. "I need Woman," he said. At first, man pictured Woman in a bowing position.

"No, she must be still more humble," said man. He showed Woman kneeling down, as though she were kneeling down in front of man.

But Woman was not the kind of person to kneel for long. She got up and began to take big strides, to show that she could keep up with man.

The man and woman had a Baby.

And they lived ever after in Peace and Contentment.

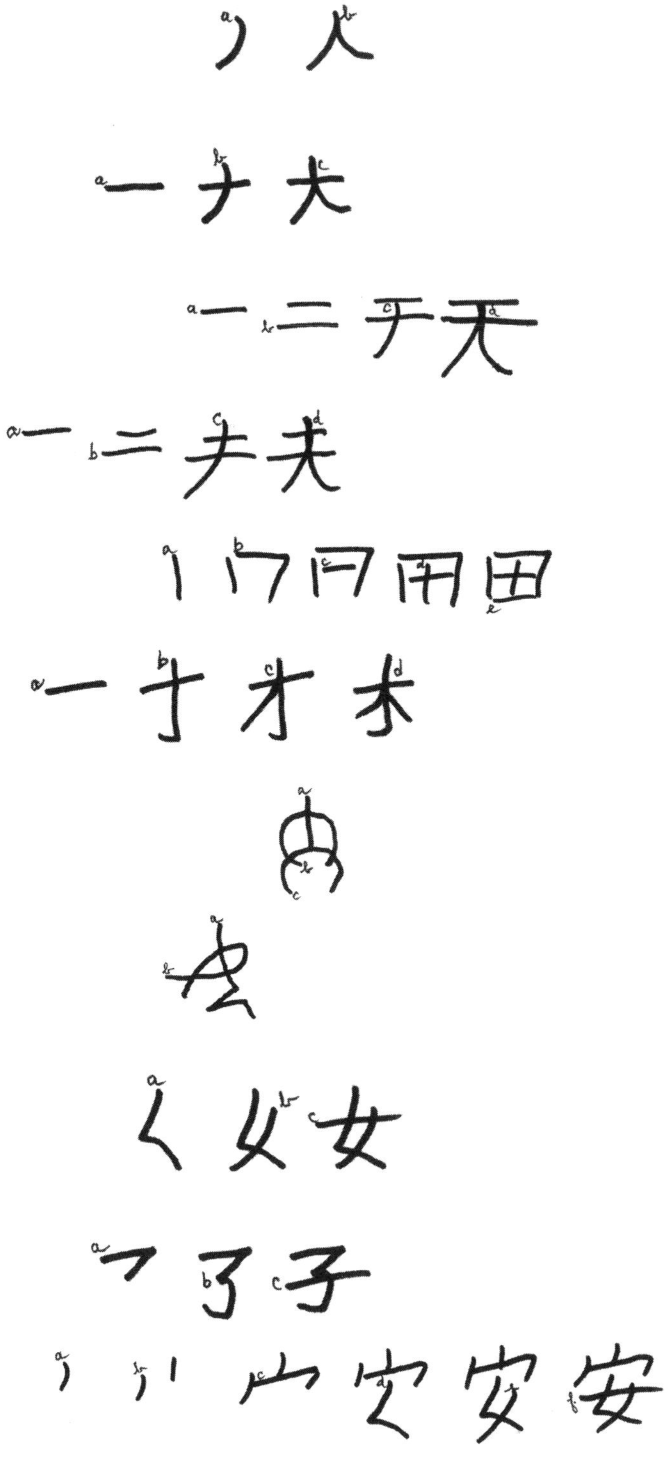

Can you see what makes up Peace and Contentment? Find the symbol for Woman, below the symbol for House or Roof.

THE ABSENT-MINDED JUDGE

Korean

The creation of Hangul, the Korean alphabet, was a stupendous cultural achievement accomplished in the fifteenth century. Before that Koreans used Chinese script. Therefore, they have inherited many of the same ways of telling stories through the use of pictures hidden in ideographs. The Society of Korean Oral Literature, affiliated with Seoul National University, has collected a number of funny drawing stories, most of them tied in with the learning of Chinese characters or letters of the Korean alphabet. Some of them are filled with sexual nuances more suited to adult telling. This short, simple tale is a good springboard for discussing the different ways we have of addressing each other, the fact that we like to use visualization to help us remember things, and that we all sometimes make mistakes!

Before telling the story, it is a good idea to have a short discussion on the ways in which we greet others politely, in public: Mister, Mrs. Miss, Ms. in English; Monsieur, Madame, Mademoiselle in French; and so on. The accepted address in Japanese is to add *san* to the surname, for example, Pellowski-*san*. In the same way, *sobang* is used in Korean, added on to the surname.

Long ago in Korea there was an absent-minded judge who was sent to a new place to hold his court. He took out a square piece of paper and called out to his new assistant: "What is your name?"

"My family name is Pae," answered the assistant. Pae means "pear" in English.

The judge wanted to remember his new assistant's name, so he lifted his writing brush, dipped it in ink, and hastily drew a picture of something round, that he thought would remind him of a pear.

The next day, the judge wanted his new assistant to come and help him. He tried to remember his name, but could not. He looked at the piece of paper. It looked like a picture of a ball, which is *kong* in Korean.

"Come here, Kong-sobang," called the judge. "Your name is Kong, isn't it?"

"No, sir. I am Pae-sobang," answered the assistant, which, of course, translates as Mr. Pear, not Mr. Ball.

The judge looked at his picture. He did not want it to be wrong. He quickly added a stroke. "Oh, I see the stem fell off of my pear overnight," he said.

To this day, in Korea, if your name is Kong, many people will call you Pae, and then you will both have a good laugh, remembering the absent-minded judge of long-ago.

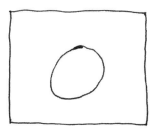

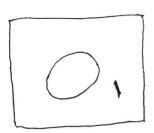

EKAKI UTA
Japanese

As mentioned in the Introduction, *ekaki uta* (picture drawing story chants) are a frequently encountered play activity among Japanese children. Each of the stories in this section has been freely adapted from the rough translations given to me by Shigeo Watanabe, and Sachiko Saionji Watanabe (no relation). I have tried to keep a bit of the rhythm of the original Japanese words, but that was not always possible. Whenever possible, I have indicated where there is a pun on the words in the original version, and I have tried to include a pun in the translated version as well. When drawing and telling these stories, try to chant the phrases in a lilting kind of sing-song manner.

After hearing and seeing a number of these stories, children often like to try doing them on their own. It takes some practice to get the figures drawn so that the parts are of a good size in relation to the whole. This might make a good short exercise in mathematical relationships. An art or number activity that children respond to with enthusiasm is to create a face or other figure using only numbers.

THE CAREFREE GIRLS

Japanese

According to most scholars in Japan who have studied the *ekaki uta*, the figure encountered most frequently is of a human face. This seems to have been the case from the earliest recorded figures. It would take an entire book to give all the variations that have been recorded. Here is a typical variant. In Japanese, there is a wonderful pun on the Japanese number eight in the phrase, "they ate honey." Luckily, this translates well by using the figure eight as a hair-bow, at the point in the story when the girl "ate" (eight) the honey.

Te-ko-chan, a little girl of Japan,

Has a best friend, Ku-ko-chan.

They ate some honey.

Their sister scolded them.

Hei-ki-de; hei-ki-de. They don't care; they don't care.

They are as carefree as two little birds.

They went to school and took a test.

They got a zero.

But everyone likes them anyway!

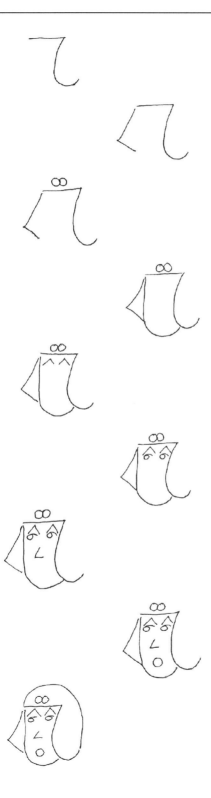

IS IT GRANDFATHER?

Japanese

Here is another common face-drawing story chant. This one was often chanted by using syllables from the *hirakana* or *katakana* methods of written Japanese, or figures from *kanji,* the written form of Japanese based on Chinese characters. To appreciate the puns in this story and in others as well, one should learn the names and figures for traditional Japanese numbers:

ichi ni san shi go (current use)
hito futa mi yo itsu (traditional use)

one	two	three	four	five
一	二	三	四	五

Take a one.

One and one are two.

Are these three wrinkles?

Is this a bald head?

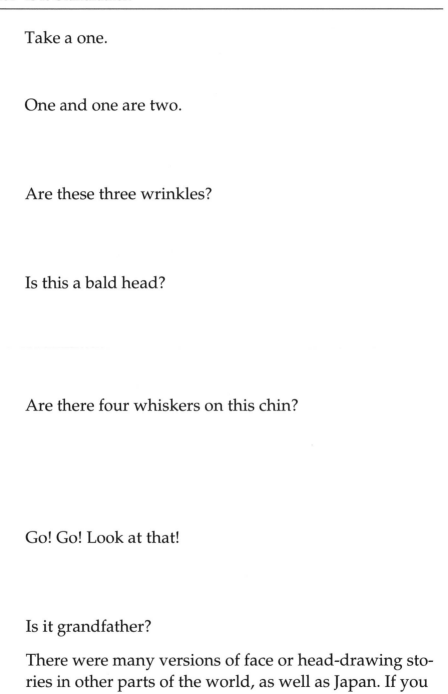

Are there four whiskers on this chin?

Go! Go! Look at that!

Is it grandfather?

There were many versions of face or head-drawing stories in other parts of the world, as well as Japan. If you are telling this to grandparents, or to senior citizens, ask if any remember such drawing stories.

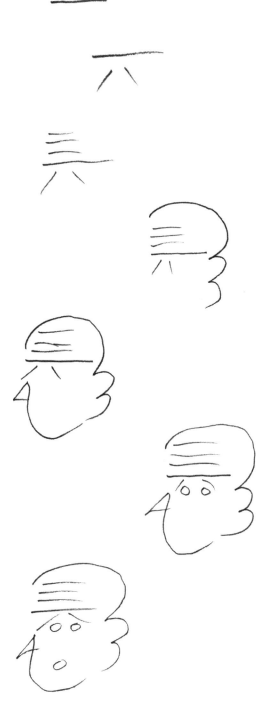

SHALL I DRAW YOUR PORTRAIT?

Japanese

The monkey appears frequently in Japanese drawing stories. In almost all cases, numbers are used to make up part of the figure. Compare this with the number quiz story in my earlier book, *The Story Vine*.

Shall I draw your portrait?

First, I must make a ten, sideways.

Then I must make a three, also sideways.

Next I must put in two small zeros.

Below them, I must put in a small hill.

Above them, I put in a curving road.

Now two doughnuts: one for you and one for me!

Now stick your tongue out because—

You are a monkey!

TO HELP YOU FEEL BETTER

Japanese

The word *maru* in Japanese means "circle." By adding *chan*, one gets the girl's name Maruchan. This name is often used in Japanese drawing stories while drawing a circle and referring to a girl at the same time.

Maruchan fell down.

She got a big bump on her head.

Her brother put a bandage around her head.

Maruchan stuck out her tongue!

Mother came and said:

"Here is some tea to help you feel better."

THE OCTOPUS

Japanese

This is one of the most popular of all *ekaki uta*. There are many versions and most Japanese children who have just learned to write can chant and draw this little story. Make sure you do six strokes of "raining." When I first started doing this, I occasionally would stop at five strokes and I was once informed by a first-grader, very solemnly, that an octopus has eight tentacles. I try to make sure I now get it right.

Three little worms came crawling along, crawling along, crawling along.

Three rice crackers were singing a song, singing a song, singing a song.

It started raining, raining, raining, raining, raining, raining [make sure you do six].

It started sleeting, sleeting, sleeting, sleeting, sleeting, sleeting, sleeting.

All of a sudden, oh, what a surprise! There was an octopus right before my eyes!

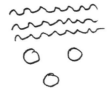

THE ONE THAT GOT AWAY

Japan

This *ekaki uta* is very popular with Japanese children because fish are very important in their diet. Also, when visiting ponds and streams, they love to capture small minnows or goldfish and take them home in a bowl or plastic bag.

Once there was a small mountain.

At the eastern foot of the mountain were three houses.

In the houses lived some farmers.

In spring they planted a garden.
They planted three rows of radishes.

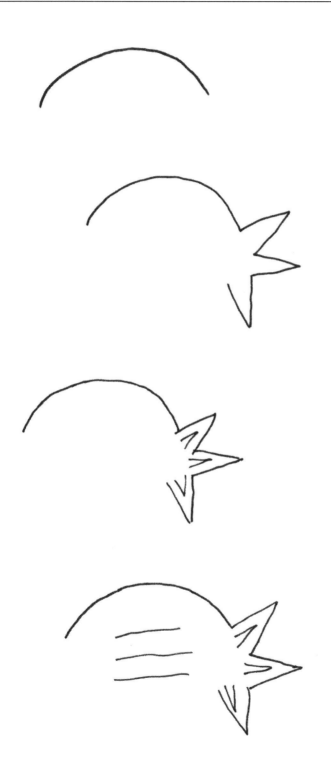

In the other direction they planted three rows of lettuces.

To the west of the garden were two ponds.

A round one—

And an oval one.

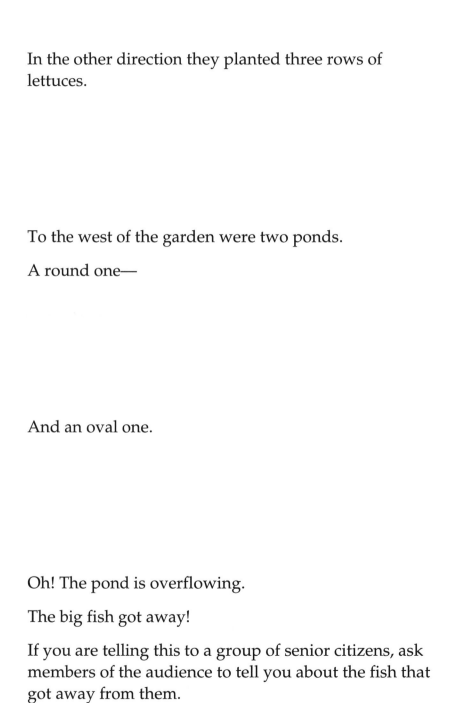

Oh! The pond is overflowing.

The big fish got away!

If you are telling this to a group of senior citizens, ask members of the audience to tell you about the fish that got away from them.

THE DUCK

Japanese

It is better not to give away the title of this at the beginning. In Japanese, *ni* is the number two (see the story IS IT GRANDFATHER? on p. 103). It can also be the word for brother. Yen are Japanese money units. If you wish to substitute dollars or cents, do so.

My two brothers

Got three yen.

They bought a small ball.

One brother asked:
"What letter do question words begin with?"

The other brother answered:
"W—for who, what, when, where, how."
"That's right. So put a W sideways, here,"
said the other brother.

And what did they have?

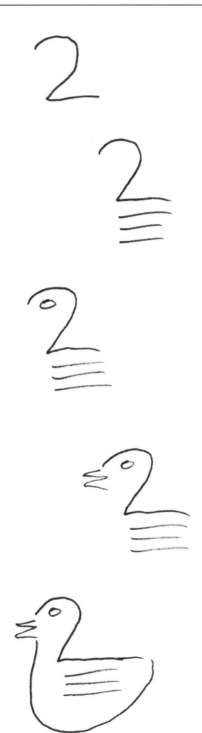

WHAT HAPPENED
AFTER THE RAIN

Japanese

This *ekaki uta* has many variations. Sometimes the pig is shown from the side; at other times it is shown facing forward, as here.

One day it rained

And it rained

And it rained.

It rained so hard, puddles began to form. A puddle formed here.

Two puddles formed here and here;

Two more puddles grew here.

The puddles overflowed and made a big puddle.

It rained more, very heavily.

The puddles overflowed again.
They made a giant puddle!

"Ee, Ee, Ee," said the pig. "I love puddles."

After doing the drawing, if you have little children in your audience who are just learning their numbers, ask them, How many ones are in the drawing? Help them count the ten ones if they cannot see them all. Then, ask them, How many zeros are in the drawing. Again, help them to count the ten zeros. [Don't forget the three in the tail.]

Then ask, When you put one and zero together, what do you get? Write out a big number ten at the bottom of your drawing.

PANDA

Japanese

Do not give the title until the end of the story. It would be good to locate a *furoshiki,* a square silk cloth used for wrapping special gifts in Japan. You could then use this story to introduce different ways of wrapping or presenting gifts in various parts of the world.

First, I put down two chopsticks.

Next, I put three beans in place.

Two of the beans are still in their pods.

I wrap them all up carefully in a *furoshiki*.

The ends of the cloth make two round bumps, at the top.

Oh, look, I have a friendly panda to give as a gift.

[Shade in eyes and ears.]

There are numerous panda picture books to use with this story. One of my favorites is a book published many years ago: *Milton the Early Riser* by Robert Kraus, illustrated by Jose Aruego (New York: Windmill Books, 1972).

THE CHEERLEADER

Japanese

Again, do not give away the story surprise by telling the title until the very end. Note that most of the numbers from one to ten can be found in this drawing. If appropriate and if time allows, ask the children in the audience, Who can find a one in the drawing? Who can find a two? and so on. Give each child a marker of a different color and ask each to come up and trace the number in your finished drawing. If you prefer to have girls instead of boys playing baseball, substitute "two sisters" in line two for "two brothers" and change the other lines as necessary.

Little Zero

Had two brothers.

They both liked to play baseball.

Older Brother was the best hitter. He was always batter number four in the line up.

There's a pitch to him. [Stroke over the down stroke in the four, making it longer, and then add the circle at the tip.]

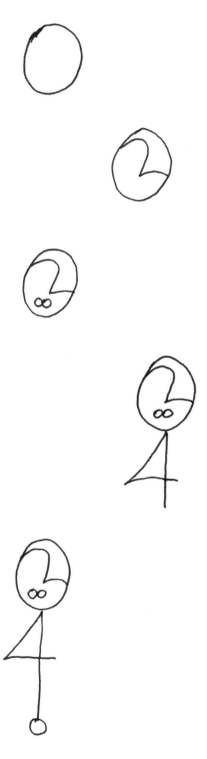

He hits a home run. [Stroke over the horizontal stroke in the four and add the circle at the end.]

The people cheer.

Rah! Rah! Rah!

Rah! Rah! Rah!

Oh, look! There is the cheerleader! [Put in sideways six for the eye.]

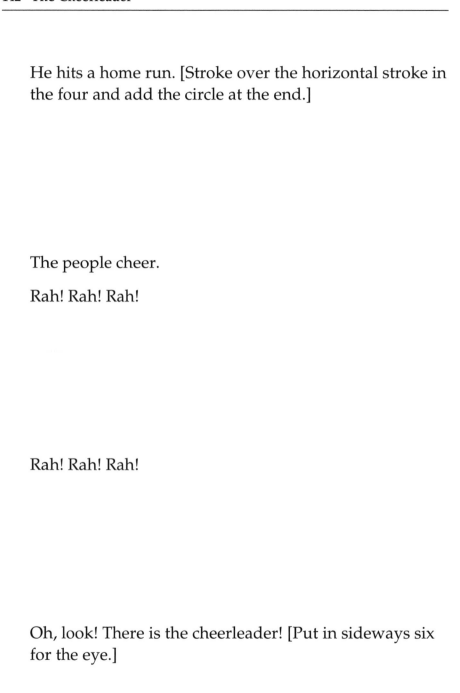

At the end of the story, one could have a discussion of the favorite sports children follow in different parts of the world. Note that it is an event in baseball that is being cheered here. One could not substitute American football, because it is not a popular sport in Japan, but soccer would be possible. Have the audience suggest appropriate actions for the drawings in figures three through six, if they were playing a sport in another part of the world. For example, in Green Bay, Wisconsin (football); in Brazil (soccer); in China (ping-pong); in Wimbledon, England (tennis); and so on. Or, if it is near the time for an Olympics, one could substitute the name of a well-known athlete. Ask the audience how the story words could be changed, so the crowd could be cheering for that athlete.

CICADA

Japanese

This story is accompanied by a very well-known song, sung in most early grades in Japanese schools. For those wishing to sing it, the music is given in Iwai (see the Bibliography). The term used for the antennae in most versions is whiskers, but use antennae if you wish to be more scientifically correct.

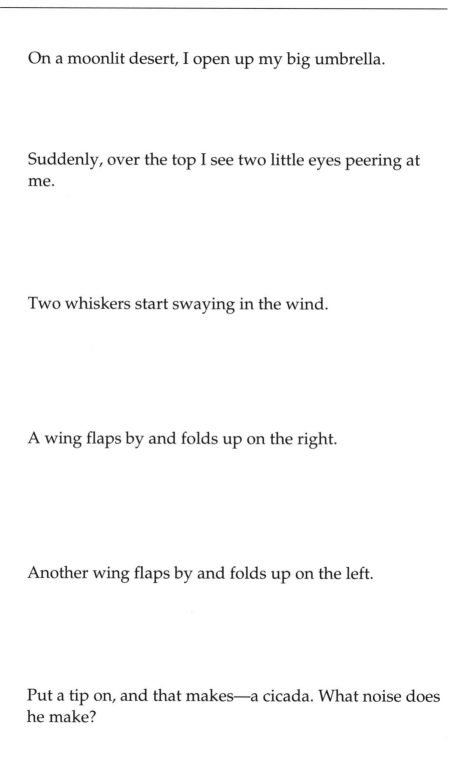

On a moonlit desert, I open up my big umbrella.

Suddenly, over the top I see two little eyes peering at me.

Two whiskers start swaying in the wind.

A wing flaps by and folds up on the right.

Another wing flaps by and folds up on the left.

Put a tip on, and that makes—a cicada. What noise does he make?

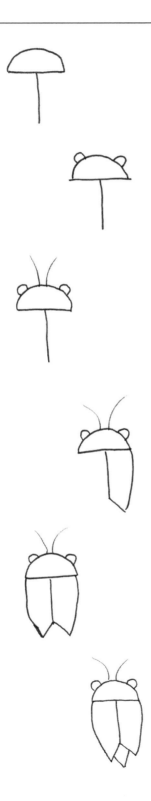

WATCH OUT!
YOU'LL TURN INTO A FROG!

Japanese

In many versions of this drawing story, the marbles are peas. However, marbles seem more appropriate here. Don't give the title to the story before telling it. I have substituted more commonly known names for the boy and girl than those generally used by Japanese children when telling and drawing. If you prefer, reverse the names and have the boy stick out his tongue at the girl, and change into a frog. You might even use this as a humorous introduction to variants on "The Frog Prince."

Ichiro was a boy in Japan.

He had two small marbles and two big marbles.

Along came Kiyoko. She asked Ichiro for some of the marbles. He would not give her any.

Kiyoko stuck out her tongue at Ichiro!

"Watch out!" said Ichiro. "You will turn into a frog."

CATERPILLAR

Japanese

    I saw this chanted by a child using green chalk on a sidewalk. Pickled plums are a Japanese delicacy. Later, I saw other versions in which the caterpillar is depicted as one long horizontal stroke with a series of short vertical strokes through it, and two round eyes, thus:

I lined up five dumplings on my plate.

On the biggest dumpling, I put two pickled plums.

Three hairs popped out of the dumpling on this side.

And three more popped out on this side.

Oh, look! If I put a hair-bow at the end, it makes a cater-pillar.

SANTA CLAUS

Japanese

Santa Claus is almost as important in modern Japanese culture as he is in North America. This drawing story could be used to find out the different choices children would make if they were inventing and drawing the story in North America. Draw the story as shown here, using colored markers on white paper: red for the hat, black outline for the white items, pink for the ears and mouth. Colored chalk could also be used, on a blackboard. Then ask the children to draw Santa and name the different foods they would see as part of the picture. This story can also be used as a felt-board story, in which case each item should be made entirely in colored felt and placed on a neutral felt background.

Maruchan, a little Japanese girl, had a red triangle hat that she loved to wear when she went out shopping with her mother.

For lunch one day, just before they went out shopping, Maruchan's mother offered her a rice ball.

"I don't want a rice ball," said Maruchan. "I want a bread roll." So her mother gave her a long bread roll instead.

They went shopping to buy food for their dinner. First, Mother bought two long *daikon*—white radishes.

Then Mother bought two pink plums and a yam—
a sweet potato.

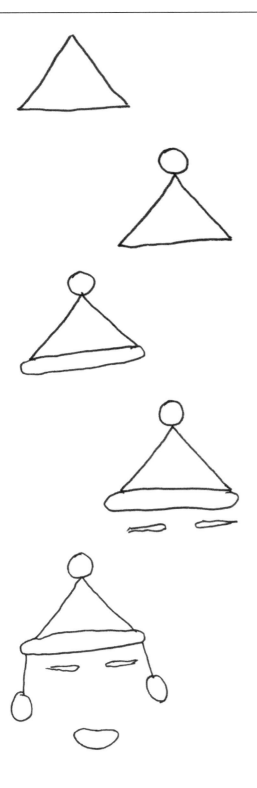

She put the rice in the pot to boil.

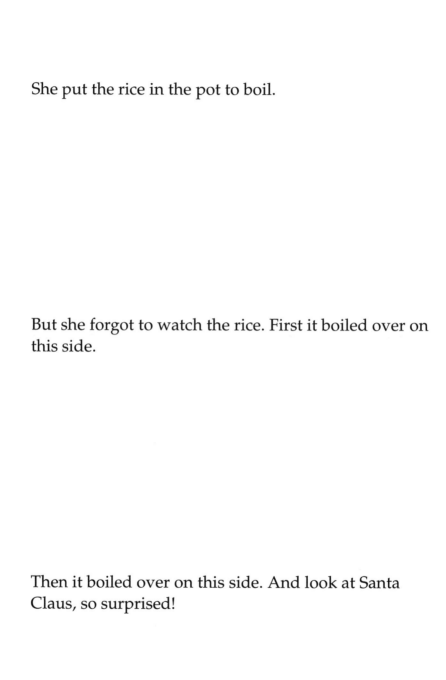

But she forgot to watch the rice. First it boiled over on this side.

Then it boiled over on this side. And look at Santa Claus, so surprised!

THE BADGER

Japanese

Badgers are very popular in much of Japanese folklore. Having grown up in the badger state of Wisconsin, I felt I must include this clever little story. It would be good to have a one yen piece to show children in the audience.

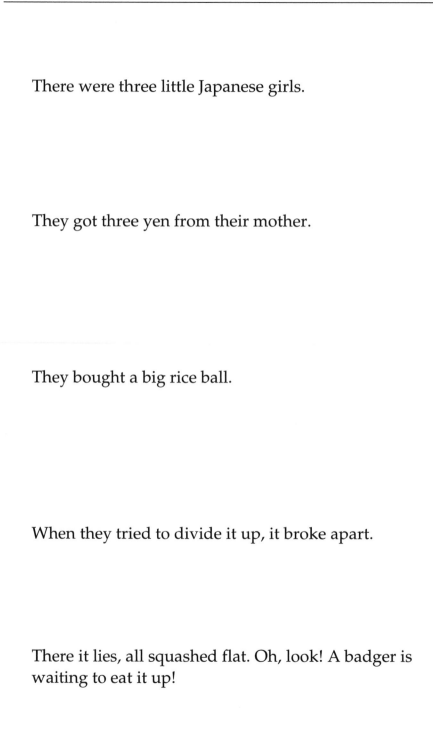

There were three little Japanese girls.

They got three yen from their mother.

They bought a big rice ball.

When they tried to divide it up, it broke apart.

There it lies, all squashed flat. Oh, look! A badger is waiting to eat it up!

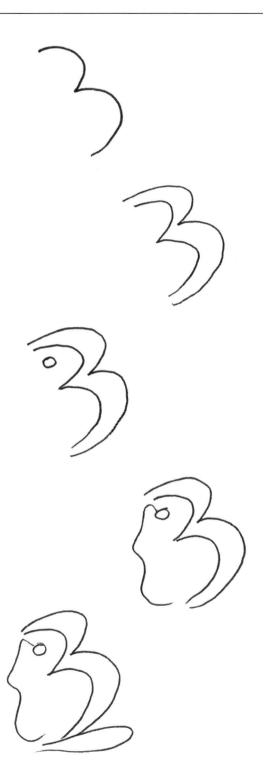

Japanese badgers look a bit different from North American badgers. Use a good animal encyclopedia to show the differences. Good books to share after this story are the Frances books by Russell and Lillian Hoban. *The Badger and the Magic Fan* by Tony Johnston, illustrated by Tomie de Paola (New York: Putnam, 1990) is a fairly typical Japanese folktale featuring the badger.

SAND STORIES
Australian Aborigine

In many Australian Aboriginal groups, stories are told while making drawings in the sand. This is usually done by women or girls. Sometimes the stories are episodes from real life. At other times they are myths. They always refer to specific places in the region of Australia that the group comes from. I owe a big debt to the late Jack Davis, who first told me about this type of storytelling and introduced me to several persons in the Alice Springs and Darwin areas of Australia who could demonstrate it.

I first recorded my way of performing this story in *The Story Vine* (New York: Macmillan, 1984). There, I suggested using a glass-bottomed box on a lighted overhead projector and showed how to construct the box. This is still an effective way of telling a sand story, because the sand flows very smoothly over the glass. However, after breaking two such boxes in my travels, I began using plastic boxes, but still placed on a lighted overhead projector.

From a one-inch deep plastic picture frame, of the type that has a slightly smaller cardboard box holding the picture in place, I discard the cardboard box and use only the plastic one. I generally use an eight by twelve–inch size. It is important to use fine art sand, available from most arts and crafts stores. The color does not matter.

Pour a thin layer of sand over the entire bottom of the box. Experiment until you find the thickness that works best for you. Use your fingertip to draw the designs. Lift the box slightly off the projector and shake the box gently from side to side to smooth the sand for the next set of designs. I indicate this by using the word "shake" at the appropriate points.

These stories can also be drawn on a flip chart or on the blackboard, but it is much better to draw them in the sand. The effect of the lighted overhead projector in a darkened room is a bit like the evening firelight that might be present when the stories are told in their original context. It is also deliciously mysterious and a bit spooky. Furthermore, this is one type of story that works well in large assemblies or auditoriums, because the pictures can be projected on a large screen or a very large white wall. I like to have the projector placed on a low table, and I sit on a lower stool, or the floor, to suggest being seated on the ground.

For a small group, one can simply make the figures in the sand while telling the story as the others watch and listen.

This is a very sacred story for many groups in Australia and should be told solemnly, and with reverence. The term "walkabout" refers to a short journey, on foot, that Australian Aborigines often make to visit a sacred site or to get away from their daily routine and connect to traditional life. "Billabong" refers to a pool of water, or a small branch of a larger river.

I taught myself some basic designs as practiced by the Walbiri, found in Nancy Munn's excellent book (see the Bibliography). However, after a visit to Australia, and a wonderful session with teachers in Alice Springs, I found I could simplify the designs because many of the women and girls drew designs that barely suggested the action. Consequently, I developed these basic design forms that are easy to remember and draw.

- For characters that are walking, a straight horizontal line is drawn.

- For a character that is standing still, the line is vertical.

- For a character seated, a small semicircle is drawn.

- The pandanus palm is drawn like the top part of an umbrella.

- Birds are the usual simple figure.

- Fish are similar to a "v" printed sideways.

- A river is a curving line.

- A billabong or lake is an oval.

- A snake is a very curvy line.

- A snake laying eggs, a spiral with dots in center. For other animals, use rough sketches of footprints, or some distinctive characteristic, such as emu's long neck.

A delightful and informative picture book to use in conjunction with these stories is *When I Was Little Like You* by Mary Malbunka, which includes both Walbiri and Luritja expressions and sand designs.

THE RAINBOW SNAKE

Australian Aborigine

In the Dreamtime, there was once a wise man named Nagacork.

One day he went for a walk along the Flying Fox River.

He made a deep billabong, a water hole. He wanted to put Jammutt, his water-shooting, sacred fish, into that billabong.

But when he went back to the small pool where he had left Jammutt, the fish was no longer there. [Shake] Nagacork was puzzled. He thought Jammutt had escaped. He began walking along the river

until he came upon some tribesmen spearing for fish.

"Have you seen Jammutt, my sacred fish?" Nagacork called out to the fishermen. But the tribesmen only laughed at him and answered: "Here, take one of these fish."

But they were ordinary fish. They were not Jammutt. [Shake]

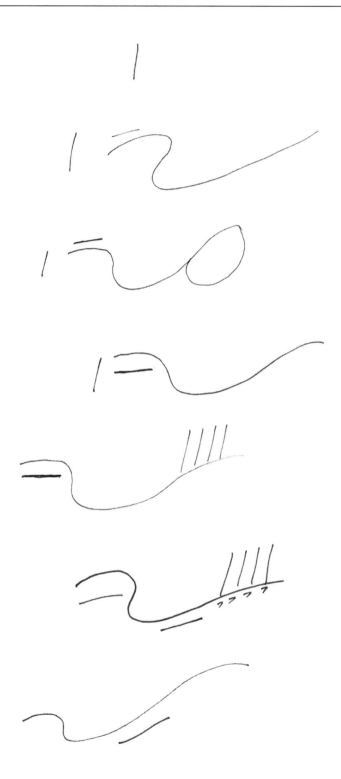

Nagacork continued on his way along the river until he came to a group of women and girls, bending over and searching for lily buds. They are delicious to eat.

"Have you seen Jammutt, my sacred fish?" he called out to them. But they were so busy looking for lily buds they did not even look up. [Shake]
Suddenly, Nagacork saw a colony of ants, crawling along the ground in a line.

He saw how they came to a coolibah tree and began to climb up it.

They went straight for a hole at the top of the coolibah tree.

Nagacork decided he must climb up the tree and see what was in that hole. [Shake]
Nagacork climbed up until he came to the hole.

He looked down, and there, he saw the bones of Jammutt, his sacred fish.

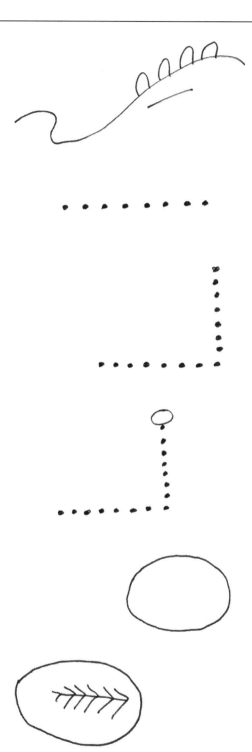

Some evil tribesmen had killed Jammutt, eaten the flesh, and thrown the bones in the hole. [Shake] Nagacork was very angry. He went back to his camp under the pandanus palms.

He sat down next to his campfire and began to call out: "I wait! I wait! I wait!"

Up in one of the trees, Dat-Dat, the green parrot, called out: "Look, Nagacork! Look what's coming from the north!"

Sure enough, there from the north came Kurrichalpongo, the great black rock snake.

[Shake]

Kurrichalpongo headed straight for the billabong that Nagacork had made for Jammutt.

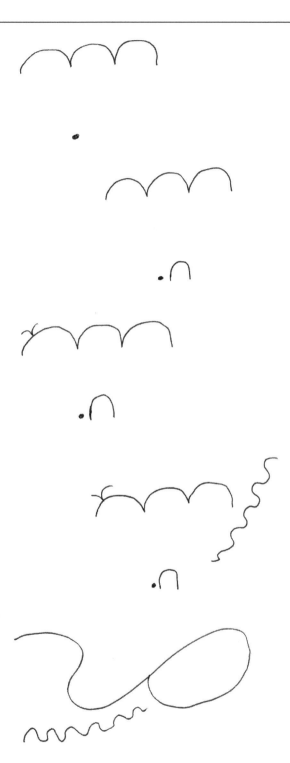

There at the billabong were some tribesmen, spearing for fish. They were among the evil tribesmen who had killed Jammutt. They wanted the billabong for their own fishing uses.

Kurrichalpongo came in from below with a rush of water.
The water rushed over the tribesmen's legs, over their waists, over their shoulders, over their heads. [Swirl sand in circles from bottom of tribesmen to top.]
Most of the tribesmen were drowned. [Shake]

Kurrichalpongo continued on her way. With her passing, she created all the features of the land of Australia. She created the great plain.

As soon as she had passed, bitter yams grew up from the ground. They grow there to this day.

[Shake]

Then Kurrichalpongo went to the desert and curled up.

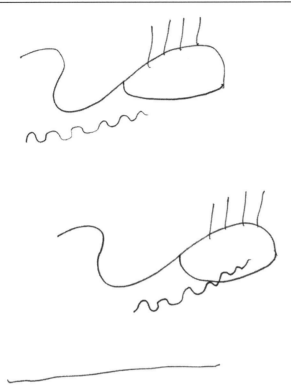

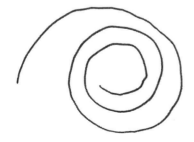

Before long, she laid a nest of many eggs and sat, curled up around them.

When the eggs hatched out, they were all rainbow snakes, sacred snakes. They went off in all directions of Australia, taking with them the wisdom of Kurrichalpongo.

[Pause, and then shake.]

Now two of those snakes went to Luralingi, where there lived two of the evil tribesmen who had killed Jammutt. The two tribesmen were out hunting and they saw the two rainbow snakes.

They shot and killed the rainbow snakes with their spears. [Make a swift line from men to snakes and then shake.]

Nagacork was sitting by his campfire.

The two tribesmen suddenly stood before him and said: "Look what we have brought you!" They threw the snakes at Nagacork's feet. Kurrichalpongo appeared again. She turned into Bolong, the giant rainbow snake.

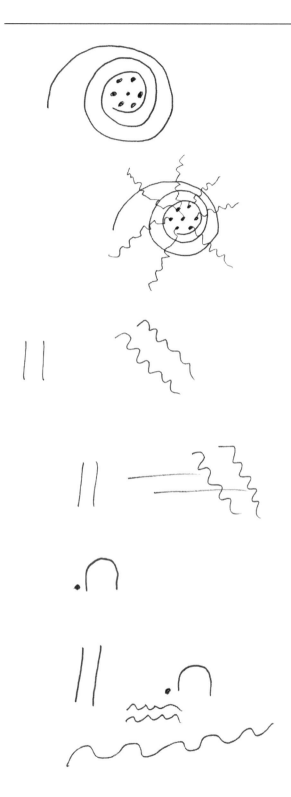

"You men should not have done that," said Nagacork sadly. "Those are rainbow snakes, sacred snakes. You will surely die for what you have done."

Bolong caused thunder and lightning and a great flood of rain. [Swirl entire picture with fingertips so sand is completely mixed up, then shake.]

The flood covered the earth. A few humans went to high ground and were saved. They became the ancestors of the original Australians.

Others changed into birds and flew away. They became the ancestors of the birds that fly around Australia today.

Still others changed themselves into fish, or water creatures. They are the ancestors of the water animals that exist today in Australia.

Some changed themselves into kangaroos, or koalas or other animals, and they scuttled away. They were the ancestors of those animals that exist today.

[Shake]

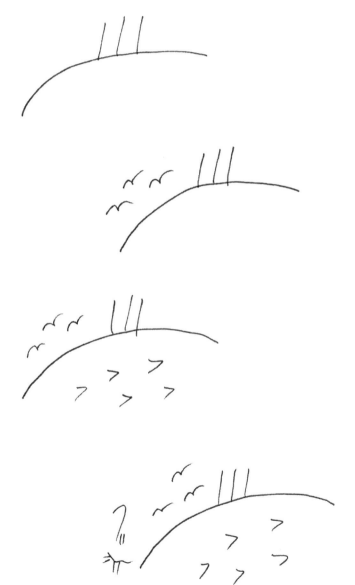

Finally, Kurrichalpongo went off to Moorinjairee. There, she met up with Nagacork and the remaining rainbow snakes. And there, in a deep hole in the ground, they all went back into the earth—first Nagacork

then Kurrichalpongo and all the rainbow snakes.

They have remained there ever since.

The Aboriginal people of Australia say they will not come back until humans can learn to live with respect for all that is around them. Only then will the Dream-time return.

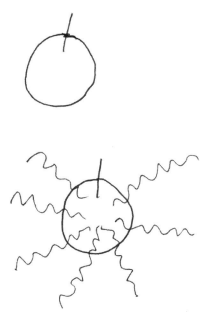

LITTLE BOY AND EMU

Nunggubuyu—Australian Aborigine

A mother and father were on walkabout with their son, Little Boy. The parents walked ahead, and Little Boy followed behind.

[Shake]

Little Boy kept throwing his spear at wild gooseberry bushes.

He called out to his mother and father every now and then to tell them he was still following them. But soon he had fallen far behind.

Now Little Boy did not know that Emu was watching him from behind the bushes.

[Shake]

Suddenly, Emu came out from behind the bushes and said: "Come here!"

But Little Boy ran away as fast as he could. Emu ran after him.

[Shake]

Little Boy jumped into a billabong. The water was too deep and too wide for Emu.

Emu ran to cut down a pandanus palm.

[Shake]

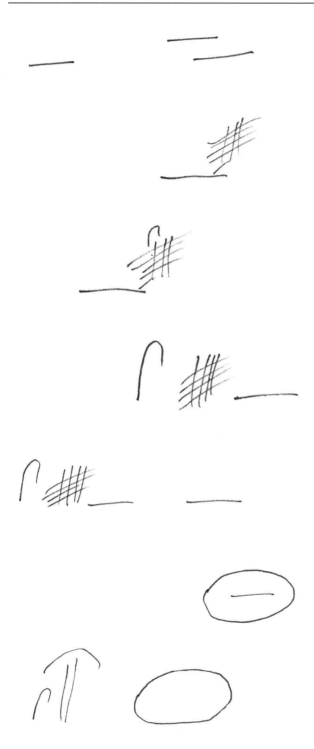

Emu took the pandanus palm to the billabong and began to drag it through the water, sideways, to see if she could catch Little Boy.

But Little Boy just took hold of the pandanus palm and got a free ride in the water. It was fun! Just before Emu pulled the tree out of the water, Little Boy let go. [Shake]

When Emu had the pandanus palm out of the water, she saw that she had caught some fish in its branches, but not Little Boy.

[Shake]

Emu continued to walk along the river, searching for Little Boy. She saw his tracks leading to a tall pandanus palm.

Up near the top of the trunk was a hole.

Emu thought she saw Little Boy's eyes shining in that hole.

[Shake]

Emu started to cut around the hole, underneath Little Boy.

"Don't cut there! Cut here!" shouted Little Boy as he knocked on the tree above his head. [Point to tree top with finger in sand.]

Emu stretched her neck. [Using fingertip, elongate Emu's neck until it reaches hole.]

Little Boy stuck his head out of the hole and bit Emu.

"Ow! Ow! Ow! Ow! Ow!" shrieked Emu. [Shake]

Emu fell down. She lay at the bottom of the tree.

Cautiously, Little Boy climbed out of the hole and ran after his parents, following their tracks as quickly as he could.

You can adapt many stories, from Australia or from other countries, and tell them by making pictures in the sand. Invent your own figures to represent places, animals, or humans.

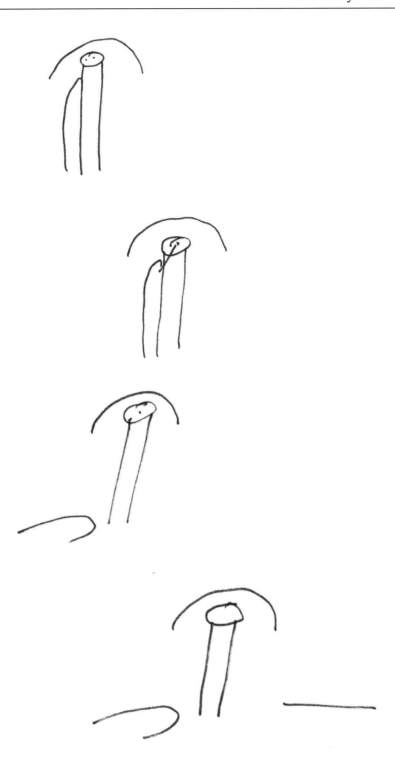

THE LITTLE GIRL
AND HER GRANDMOTHER

Napaskiak, Yuk

One of the favorite playthings of certain indigenous children's groups in Alaska and the Bering Strait area is a knife! Not a sharp knife for cutting, but a storyknife. In the olden days, storyknives were made of carved bone or tusk. In more recent times, children use ordinary metal table knives. Storyknifing is most common among young girls, but small boys do it as well. In winter, the pictures are drawn in the snow. In the other seasons, the pictures are made in patches of squishy mud or sand that can be patted into a smooth surface. The pictures vary from locale to locale, and from child to child. Here are some of the more commonly used human figures among the Napaskiak people:

Child   Adult   Older person, usually grandmother

Each time a character speaks, a stroke or quotation marks are added above the figure representing that character. Sometimes the character is erased by smoothing over the snow, mud, or wet sand, either to indicate that the character has moved on to other action or to make room for another design.

When telling this story outside in the snow or wet sand or mud, use an ordinary table knife. For inside telling, use chalk on a blackboard, or marker on a large flip chart on an easel. Or you could adapt the designs and use the sand technique mentioned in the Australian Aboriginal stories.

Build up the suspense by slowing down and making your voice softer at the point where the little girl is climbing the hill.

I have indicated where to erase, if you are using the blackboard or sand story method. If you are using markers on a large paper pad placed on an easel, simply flip to the next piece of paper.

193

Once, long ago in Alaska, there was an old-style house. It had a round entry room attached at one side. There was a passageway that went from the entry room into the house. There was a firepit for warming in the entryway and a firepit for cooking in the main part of the house.

Along the inside walls of the house were sleeping benches. There were also cupboards for food, and utensils and clothing.

In that house lived a grandmother and her granddaughter.

Not far from the house was a river. In the distance, beyond the river, was a high hill.

One spring day the grandmother said to her granddaughter: "Let's go out and cut grass."

"All right," agreed the granddaughter. [Put the strokes over their heads, indicating they have spoken.]

They went to the side of the river and began to cut grass. When they had finished, the granddaughter looked up. In the distance she saw the high hill.

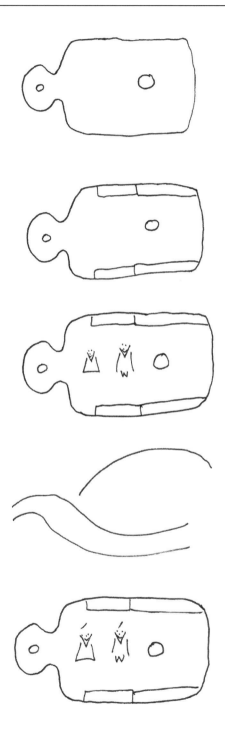

"I want to go to the top of that hill," she said. [Stroke over her head.]

"No, you must not go there," said her grandmother. "It is dangerous." [Stroke over grandmother's head. Erase or flip to next sheet.]

One day in summer the grandmother and the girl went to the berry bushes that grew along the river. They picked all the berries they could find. When they had finished, the granddaughter again looked off toward the hill.

"I want to go to the top of that hill," she said. [Stroke over her.]

"Don't go there. It is dangerous," repeated the grandmother." [Stroke over her. Erase or flip to next sheet.]

In the fall, the grandmother and her granddaughter took their kayaks down to the river. They paddled their kayaks to a part of the river where fish were plentiful. They fished until they had enough to last for the winter.

"Now I am going to climb to the top of that hill," said the granddaughter. [Stroke over her head.]

"I told you many times before. Don't go there. It is dangerous," insisted the grandmother. [Stroke over her head. Erase or flip to next sheet.]

Winter arrived, and with it came a blanket of snow. The granddaughter and grandmother were sitting in their house.

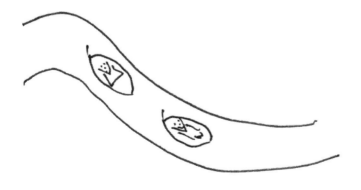

"I'm going out to do some storyknifing," said the grand-daughter. [Stroke over her.]

"Don't go too far," said her grandmother. [Stroke over her.]

The granddaughter left the house. She drew some pictures in the snow near the house. Soon, that part of the snow was covered with her tracks.

"I need some fresh snow," said the granddaughter.

She walked down to the river and because it was frozen, she could walk across it. There, on the other side of the river, was the hill she had always wanted to climb.

"Grandmother says it is dangerous, but I don't think it is so dangerous," she said to herself. "All I see is a snowy hill." [Stroke over her. Erase or move to next sheet.]

The girl climbed up the hill part way. She passed a clump of fallen branches. Whirr! Whirr!

Something flew out of the branches.

"It is only some birds," she said aloud. [Stroke over her.]

She continued climbing the hill. Suddenly, a white streak shot past her.

"It is only a snowshoe hare," she said.

[Stroke over her. Erase or move to next sheet.]

She walked higher and higher until she reached the very top of the hill.

"Eeeoww!" A terrible howl filled the air. The girl did not see a thing, but she jumped, turned around, ran down the hill [make dots along path she takes] and ran back to her home as fast as she could.

[Erase or move to next sheet.]

When she got to her home, grandmother was waiting for her. Now what do you suppose it was that frightened her on top of that hill?

A wonderful book to use in conjunction with this story is *Tundra Mouse* by Megan McDonald, illustrated by S. D. Schindler (New York: Orchard Books, 1997). Each page of this illustrated Yup'ik folktale shows the action in ordinary pictures, and in the margin of each illustration are the designs that children would use when "storyknifing" in snow or mud. After telling the story once or twice, and showing the storyknifing designs, see if the audience can remember and reproduce any of the designs. This could be done in chalk or with marker, or, if you and the group are adventurous, in a fresh snow bank.

WHAT CAN HAPPEN IF YOU FALL INTO A HOLE

South Africa

Each time I have visited school or libraries in various African countries in the past, I have asked both children and adults whether they knew any drawing stories. Only recently, during the 29th Congress of the IBBY in Cape Town did I encounter a group of children who knew some drawing stories that were not variants of the first two stories in this collection. Lisa Nell was the first one to draw and tell me this little story.

There was once a man who went out for a walk.

He fell into a big hole.

He got two bumps on his head.

He continued walking, and fell into an even bigger hole.

He got two more bumps on his head.

Look at that! He turned into a bear!

HANDKERCHIEF STORIES FROM EUROPEAN TRADITIONS

Introduction

Almost forty years ago, I heard and saw my first handkerchief story. While visiting friends and sharing stories in Munich, Germany, a grandparent in a neighboring family told a story using the mouse figure, shown later in this section. At the time, I thought it was a type of story developed by that person to tell to his grandchildren. But after talking about it a bit, I realized it was just one of a number of handkerchief "trick" stories that had been passed on in families.

After researching the handkerchief a bit, I found information in various histories of the handkerchief that these stories, accompanied by figures made with the handkerchief, were common throughout Europe, but especially in Germany and the Netherlands. Usually, they had been learned in the last decades of the nineteenth century or the early decades of the twentieth.

The children's book author Alta Halverson Seymour, when writing the book *Galewood Crossing*, which is partly based on her family's history, cites a very unusual use for handkerchief stories. In Chapter Sixteen of that book, "Company for Thanksgiving," she describes a sharing of handkerchief figures and stories with a group of Native Americans who had come to the rescue of one of the daughters in the family.

I searched in vain through folklore journals for references to this type of story, but could find none. I did not locate the earlier items mentioned in the bibliography until much later. Curiously, when I would ask older European persons if they remembered such stories, many said they did, but could give me no examples. However, I did find one elderly man in Japan who knew the mouse figure and could tell a kind of story with it.

On a trip to Netherlands in 1985, I spoke at a Dutch Library Association meeting about different types of storytelling, and mentioned my search for handkerchief stories. Quite a number of persons in the audience came up afterward and volunteered to show me figures. But it was Cecile Beijk van Daal (who invited me to her home near Eindhoven), and her many family members, who were able to introduce me to quite a few figures and bits of story. I worked these up in English versions, adding to each little story as seemed appropriate

I began telling them all over the world. Subsequently, I tracked down a number of printed references to handkerchief figures, but most of them did not give any story. The earliest I located, in terms of publication, was the Frikell book, edited by W. H. Cremer. This also seems to be the earliest printed use of the term "hanky panky" to describe any type of trick figure or magical trick. That book, which was an amateur magician's handbook in the nineteenth century, includes only three handkerchief "tricks" that one was supposed to flesh out with a story.

The *Oxford English Dictionary* tentatively cites the term "hanky panky" as a derivative of hocus pocus and gives it these definitions: "legerdemain, trickery, double dealing." The first printed use of it with this meaning seems to have been in the magazine *Punch* in 1841. Since the handkerchief figures were known well before that it seems to me much more likely that the term came about precisely because of these "tricky" figures.

By the end of the nineteenth century, the term was definitely also associated with these figures, and not just general trickery. And this has remained true throughout the twentieth century, as can be shown by the publication of at least three books with that term in the title. Most of them were probably inspired by the title of the Frikell book, which was reproduced several times in the century.

It was interesting to note that a recent television version of the novel *Doctor Zhivago*, showed a scene of Uncle Kolya telling the mouse story to little Yuri Zhivago, after his adoption following the death of his mother. So the figures are still being kept alive through modern media.

My personal preference is for keeping them alive by sharing them with small groups of listeners in family and school and library story hours. They are easy to teach to parents and grandparents and make ideal fillers to insert between longer stories in family story hours.

I like to tell these by showing the handkerchief figure as it progresses on a large piece of pale-colored felt, clipped or taped on an easel. The handkerchief sticks to the felt because of the nap. (One often has to explain this to little children, because they can't figure out why the handkerchief stays up without glue or tape.) I use a typical man's handkerchief, usually of the plain white variety.

My introduction almost always begins thus:

Who knows what this is called? [Hold up handkerchief.] Yes, it's called a handkerchief. "Kerchief" means "a cover cloth," so this is a hand cover cloth. Did you know there is a story hiding in this hand-kerchief? A long, long time ago, when your great, great, great, great, great, great grandparents were growing up, they didn't have tissues. They didn't have handkerchiefs either. If they needed to blow their noses, do you know what they did? The just leaned over, blew their noses, and then wiped them with their fingers, like this. [Demonstrate by miming this action.] Yuck!

Only princes and princesses and people of the court had handker-chiefs. And people who acted in the theater. But slowly, slowly, ordi-nary people began to use the handkerchief. Mothers and fathers, grandmothers and grandfathers, wanted to introduce its use to their children and grandchildren, so they could be more polite. They in-vented many funny, tricky figures, and little stories to go along with the figures. This made the children more accepting of the handker-chief. Many of the stories end up with the figure hiding in a pocket, because that is what parents wanted to have their children remem-ber: always have a handkerchief hiding in your pocket. Here is one of those stories.

THE PUZZLED PROFESSORS

Dutch

This story/rhyme was given to me by many persons in the Netherlands, but I have used the version remembered by Cecile Beijk's aunt. I give it here in Dutch first, for those who wish to say it in the original, and then in my English translation. The figure can be found in most of the books cited in the bibliography. This is perfect for audience participation. Make seven "professor" figures out of seven handkerchiefs and have seven audience members put them on the fingertips of one hand and act out the story. Make the basic figures by knotting one corner of the handkerchief, leaving about one inch of the corner tip sticking up.

Dames en heren! Zeven Professoren!
Als heel de wereld stokvis was,
En elke boom en gas.
Als zee en meer en waterplas,
Eens louter haring was—
Waarmee lesten wij dan onze dorst?
Over dit gewichtig vraagstuk hebben zeven professoren zich
zeven dagen lang zitten te krabben achter hun oren.

Ladies and gentlemen!
If the whole world was of dried fish,
And every tree a gas.
If sea and lake and creek
Was only salted herring—
With what would we quench our thirst?
About this important problem seven professors have
spent seven long days scratching behind their ears.

[Have the persons holding the figures reach up with their thumbs and pretend to scratch behind the knots.]

RABBIT STORY

European

This can be done with either a handkerchief or a white napkin. A Dutch librarian once told me that when, as a child, he refused to eat everything on his plate, his grandfather would say something like this: "That's too bad, then, because unless you clear your plate, I can't tell you about the rabbit." When his plate was cleaned of food, his grandfather would then tell him rabbit stories, while making the figure with his napkin. Other Dutch persons reported that a version of this story was used to remind them to always have a handkerchief in their pockets, in the days before tissues.

If you were to go not far from here, you would find a small hill.
[Put handkerchief, folded in half, on felt.]

If you would dig at the bottom of that hill— [Fold over about one inch at bottom.]

And dig some more—
[Fold over another inch at bottom.]

and dig again—
[Fold over one more inch at bottom.]
you would find a soft, warm, snug little den.

[Fold figure at midpoint, making sure the folds made above are on *outside* of figure, and then flip the figure so that the hill point is facing down and becomes the opening to the den; wiggle a finger or two in the den when you are saying the words.]

In that den there lived a soft

[Grasp the figure as shown, with the thumb holding down the two ends, no more than three inch from the tip ends, and the hill point falling loosely behind the fingers, making sure the hilltop is pointing out, in the same direction as your fingertips.]

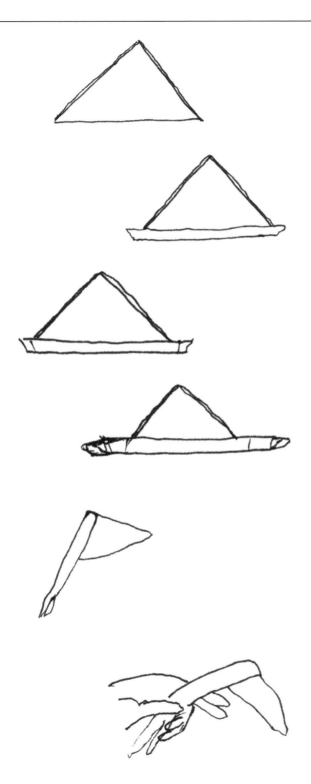

sweet

[Bring the hill part and the cuff from the back of the fingers through the space between and middle finger and ring finger and hold it in place with your thumb.]

dear

[Bring the hill point around and through the *back* of the space where your index and middle finger enter the handkerchief, at the knuckles. Tuck the points in as much as you can.]

sweet and cuddly

[Gently slide out your index and middle fingers from the space they were in, making sure you do not dislodge the hill tips you have just placed there and then in the space where your index and middle fingers once were, tuck in the folded cuff part.]

white rabbit!

[Push in the folded cuff part as far as it will go into the space once occupied by your index and middle fingers and separate the ears so they are clearly visible to the audience.]

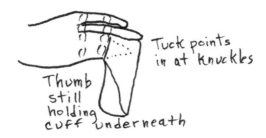

Tuck points
in at knuckles

Thumb
still
holding
cuff underneath

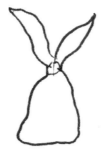

Now he was not an ordinary rabbit. Oh, no! He was a pocket rabbit. Every day he came hopping out of his den, looking for the pocket of a young lady or gentleman.

[Imitate hopping motion with rabbit figure and hop toward child in front row who has a clearly visible pocket somewhere on his clothing.]

"Here is a fine young gentleman," said the rabbit. "I want to spend the day in his pocket." And he hopped into that pocket as snug as can be and spent the day there, with his ears sticking out.

[Place rabbit in clearly visible pocket of a young boy in front row, gently motioning him to stand up and face the audience, showing rabbit with his ears sticking out of the pocket.]

At night, rabbit hopped out and went back to his den.

[Take rabbit out of child's pocket and motion for him to sit down.]

The next day rabbit went looking for another pocket where he could spend the day. This time he found a young lady with a fine pocket. "I want to spend the day with her," said the rabbit, and he hopped into her pocket, leaving his ears sticking out.

[Pop rabbit figure in pocket of girl child and make her stand facing audience, again, with ears sticking out of the pocket.]

Every day that rabbit went looking for a new pocket to spend the day, until one day, the young lady said suddenly: "Oh, dear me! I have to sneeze!" She suddenly took hold of rabbit, pulled him by the ears, and— Ka-choo! She had a handkerchief!

[Pull rabbit by the ears until he comes apart and makes a handkerchief.]

THE JUMPING MOUSE

European

Do not give away the title of this story before telling it. It seems to be the most prevalent figure used in handkerchief stories. After I had learned it from various members of Cecile Beijk's family, I found it mentioned in some early histories of the handkerchief, and in the article in *St. Nicholas Magazine* (1882), where the figure starts out the same as is shown here, but ends up as a ball; another version is given and comes out as a rabbit, but looking similar to the mouse shown in this book, rather than the rabbit head. The figure is described in most of the later books and articles, usually as a mouse. None of them give real stories associated with the figure.

I have also encountered this figure among Sunday School teachers, in certain parts of Japan, and among older immigrant populations from Central Europe whose descendants live in the Midwest of the United States. It seems to have been told more by men than women, because they liked showing how they could make the mouse figure creep up the long sleeves of their suit jackets, which had a nap that allowed them to create this effect. But the jumping action was always mentioned at the end.

My story is made up of bits and pieces of various performances of this story that I have observed over the years, plus my own performances before hundreds of groups throughout the world. Perhaps the most unusual was in Thailand in 1993, when doing storytelling workshops for Somboon Singkamanen of Srinakharinwirot University. One of the many places she had arranged for me to tell stories was at a kind of summer camp for boys. I took out my handkerchief, ready to begin a bit of its history, and then tell this story, only to have more than one hundred boys in the audience whip out their handkerchiefs, ready to imitate me in learning how to do the figure so they could become future handkerchief storytellers!

[Begin by having the handkerchief spread out on a flat table, or on a felt cloth hung up on an easel.]

I was asleep in my room one night, when down in my kitchen I heard a noise. I went down to investigate, and there on my kitchen table I saw my handkerchief spread out. I had not left it like that the night before. I was ready to pick up my handkerchief, when I saw something that seemed to be moving under it.

I wanted to see what that was, so I folded up one half of the handkerchief. I could see nothing, but I could feel something wiggling. It seemed to come from inside the handkerchief.

I am going to catch that wiggling thing, I said to myself. I folded over one tip toward the middle. Nothing there.

I folded over the other tip toward the middle. Nothing there.

But I could still feel the thing wiggling.

I started to fold up the bottom of the bottom of the handkerchief. I folded once. [Fold up about 1 inch.]

I folded twice. [Fold up another inch.]

I folded three times. [Fold up another inch.]

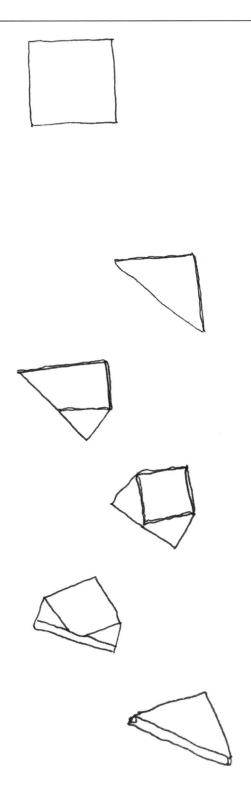

Oh! I could really feel the thing wiggle! I decided to catch that wiggly thing by folding it tightly inside the handkerchief.

[Carefully flip entire figure over to other side.]

I folded one side tightly over the middle.

Then I folded the other side over the middle. [There should be about one third in each part folded over; bottom part is called the cuffed part.]

I tucked the top tips in tight.

[Fold the cuffed part up once, creating a kind of pocket toward the front; tuck the upper tips down into this pocket, as tightly as possible.]

Oh! I could really feel that wiggly thing, trying to get out. I decided to roll it up tight so it could not get away. I rolled it.

[Turn figure in other direction. Place your thumbs into left and right sides of the pocket created on opposite side of figure from where you tucked in the points. Place your index and middle fingers behind the roll. With a kind of upward rolling motion of your thumbs, turn the figure inside out.]

I rolled it tighter!

[Again, put thumbs in pocket, and repeat upward rolling motion, turning figure inside out.]

I rolled it still tighter!

[For third time, put thumbs on either side of pocket and repeat upward motion, turning the figure inside out.]

Oh! What was that? A tail appeared!

[Separate one of the two ends that now has shown up and pull it out gently, just enough to imply a tail.]

Then, on the other end, there appeared a wee, whiskered head with two tiny ears and two beady eyes!

[Separate the tip on the other end of the figure, pulling it out a bit further.]

[Pull that second tip apart and tie it in a knot, creating the head and two tiny ears. This takes a bit of practice.]

It was a little white mouse!

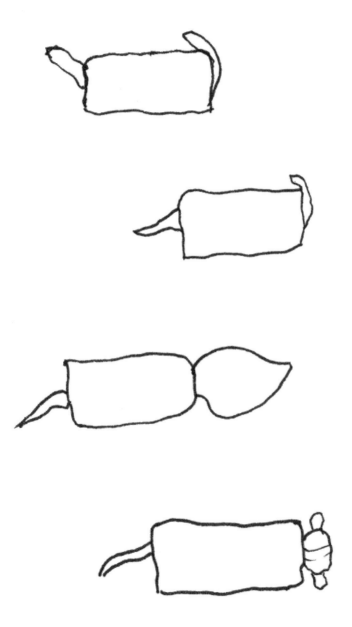

The mouse looked at me. I looked at him. All of a sudden, he gave a jump!

[Throw mouse at one of the audience members.]

He scared me, just like that. But then, I picked him up [take mouse back from audience member] and I made him my pet. [Stroke mouse along back. At this point, show tricks you can make mouse do, such as crawl along your shirt or jacket sleeve.]

I always kept mouse in my pocket, and then, if I suddenly needed to sneeze or blow my nose, I would just take mouse out of my pocket, pull him by the tail—I had a handkerchief again.

THE BABY SURPRISE

European and North American

This figure is one that seems to have survived the longest among certain populations in North America. Although it was probably brought here by Central European immigrant families, it seems to be found among all groups, particularly those with strong Sunday School traditions for young children. It was used to pacify the children and keep them quiet during Sunday school or church services. When Cecile Beijk was doing this figure for me, she sang a Dutch song while making it. Her daughter came in and reminisced on how much she had loved it, when she was mildly ill and in bed for the day, her mother or some other person in the household would make her many sets of twin babies and spread them all around her on the bed.

I have invented this story from fragments that I heard from many persons who recognized the figure and told me how it was used in their childhood. When doing this for small groups of children, I like to have enough sets of "twin babies in the cradle" made in advance so that I can give one to each child to rock for a few moments.

227

There was once a husband and wife who wanted more than anything else to have a child. They waited and waited, but no child came. They prayed to special saints. At last, the wife said: "Husband, we are going to have a child!"

What joy! How happy they were! They began to prepare everything for that child. The husband made a little cradle out of wood.

The wife made small garments and knitted soft blankets.

The husband then carved a small wooden bowl and spoon, and some toys. At last, everything seemed ready for that child.

[While listing all the preparations slowly, gently make two rolls, one on each side. Each should be about the size of a fat cigar, and they should meet in the middle.]

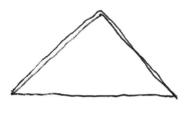

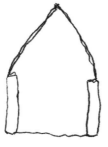

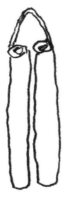

But when that baby arrived, what a surprise!

[Turn entire figure over carefully, making sure that rolls do not fall apart.]

It wasn't one baby that arrived!

[While holding down bottom tip with one hand, gently pull top tip of the handkerchief down with the other hand, until it completely covers the bottom part of figure.]

It was twins! And here they are, in their cradle!

[Grasp entire figure with hand and turn over. It is important to do this carefully, so as not to have the "babies" inside fall apart. Then gently take hold of each tip and rock the "cradle" while showing the "twins" inside.]

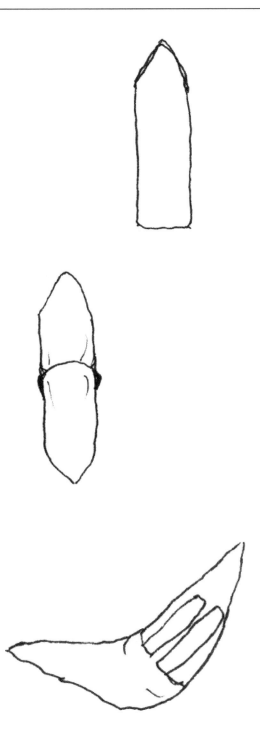

THE PEASANT'S
CLEVER DAUGHTER

European

This is not a traditional handkerchief story, but one in which I combined an old riddle story with the handkerchief, because it seemed very appropriate. You will need five handkerchiefs in all to tell the story, or one handkerchief and four triangle-shaped pieces of white cloth. (Make sure they are the correct size so that they create a square when placed on each side of the knotted handkerchief.) If telling it to a small group, simply spread the handkerchiefs on a table. If you are telling it to a larger group and you wish to show it on a felt-board, substitute the triangles of cloth and place them on each side of the knotted handkerchief figure.

I like to use this during family story hours, or with parent groups, as a pleasant introduction to a talk on the importance of reading. When telling this to children in the middle grades, I usually ask if one of the audience would come up and place the triangles on the handkerchief in such a way as to prove that the plot will be doubled. I usually explain that this is a riddle known since the time of Pythagoras, the ancient Greek philosopher and mathematician.

There was once a wealthy lord who had much land and many animals. He needed help and called a peasant farmer to his manor house.

"I will give you a square plot of land for yourself, your wife and any family you have, if you come to work for me" said the lord of the manor. [Hold up handkerchief.] "And if you do your work well, after some years I will give you more land."

The peasant farmer agreed. He and his wife built a small house on their square plot. After a year, they had their first child, a daughter. In her honor, they planted a tree in one corner of their plot. [Make knot in one corner of handkerchief.]

In two more years, they had a second child, a son. In his honor they planted a second tree, in a second corner of their plot. [Make a second knot, in a second corner of the handkerchief.]

After a few more years, they had a third child, another daughter. They planted a tree in her honor, in a third corner of their plot. [Make a knot in another corner of the handkerchief.]

"I am going to ask the lord of the manor for more land," said the peasant farmer. He promised to give us more land if we worked hard for him." He went to the manor house, but the servants who were guarding the front door would not let him in. He could not even present his case to the lord of the manor.

After another few years, the farmer and his wife had another child, a second son. In his honor they planted a tree in the last corner of their square plot. They now had a tree in each corner. [Make knot.]

"See here," said the wife. "We work very hard for the lord. You must go to him and insist that he give us more land, or we shall not do any more work."

The farmer went off to the manor, and this time, he was fortunate that there were no servants guarding the door. He walked right in and spoke to the lord.

"You promised me more land if we worked hard for you. I have a growing family. We need more land."

"Ah, yes," said the lord, and he took out his handkerchief. "You are the one to whom I gave that square plot of land. I notice that you now have four trees planted, one in each corner. Why did you do that?"

"In honor of my four children," answered the peasant farmer. "I planted one for each of them."

Now the lord was a jolly fellow who liked tricks and riddles. He took his handkerchief, made a knot in each corner, and held it out to the peasant farmer, saying: "Yes, I notice you do work hard, and you deserve more

land. I will give you more land, but I will let you double the size of your plot, if you can answer this three-part riddle. You must keep your plot square, you must keep the trees where they are, and the trees must stay at the edge of your plot. Here, go home and bring me the answer tomorrow, in cloth." The lord handed the handkerchief to the peasant farmer.

When he got home, his wife asked: "Did you get more land?"

"I did, and I didn't," replied the farmer. "We will definitely get more land, but if we can answer the lord's riddle, we can double the size of our plot."

"Give me the riddle," said his wife. "I am very good at riddles."

The peasant held up the handkerchief with the four knots.

"This is our plot. The knots are our trees. The lord says we can double our plot, if we keep it square, if we keep the trees where they are, and if we keep the trees at the edge of our plot. I have not been able to figure it out," said the farmer.

His wife took the handkerchief in her hands and pondered the problem, but she could not find the answer to the three-part riddle.

Just then, their oldest daughter came home and she stepped forward, saying, "Father, I know the answer."

"You do! Tell me, quickly," said her father.

The daughter took the handkerchief from her father's hands, and went in search of more cloths from the kitchen. She folded them carefully and then said: "You must ask for a piece of land shaped like this on the north side of our plot. [Spread out handkerchief with knots and place another handkerchief, folded three times in triangle shape, at top. Or, if using a felt board, place a cloth cut in appropriate triangle shape and size at top.]

Then you must ask for a piece of land of the same size and shape on the east side of our plot. [Place a handkerchief or cloth of same triangle size on right side of figure.]

Then ask for a piece of land of the same size and shape to the west of our plot. [Place still another handkerchief or cloth, of same triangle size, on left side of figure.]

Finally, ask for a piece of land of the same size and shape to the south of our plot. [Place last handkerchief or cloth of same triangle size at bottom of figure.]

As you see, the plot stays square, the trees stay where they are, and they remain at the edge of our plot."

"Daughter, I am a *dummkopf*. How did you know those answers?" asked her father.

"No, father, you are not a *dummkopf*, because you allowed me to go to school, and I read the answer to those riddles in a book," answered the daughter.

And that is how the peasant and his family doubled their plot of land overnight, all because their daughter had learned to read. [To prove a doubling of the plot, place triangles with tips in the center.]

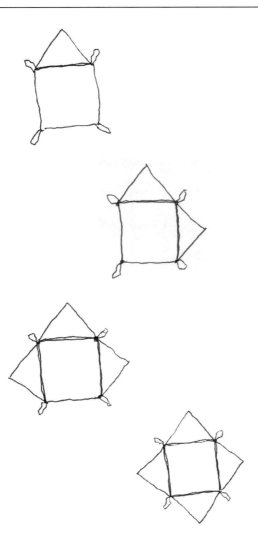

SOURCES OF THE DRAWING STORIES

The Black Cat

This is my own version, but it is based mostly on the two versions published in the *Journal of American Folklore,* 1897, p. 80 and p. 322. They had been submitted to the journal by Maud G. Early and Ida C. Craddock, respectively. Both remembered them from childhood. Charles Ludwidge Dodgson's version appears in the appendix of *The Diaries of Lewis Carroll,* vol. 2, edited by Roger Lancelyn Green. It is called "Mr. T and Mr. C." For numerous versions from the Nordic countries, plus excellent source notes (in Swedish), see the two volumes compiled by Per Gustavsson.

The Wolves, the Goats and the Kids

This is based on an oral version of the German children's book writer Fritz Muhlenweg and a print version pointed out later to me by the writer Hans Baumann. While visiting the Baumann home in 1959, I happened to do the drawing story of "The Black Cat" for the little daughter in the house, Veronica. Herr Baumann mentioned that his friend, Fritz Muhlenweg, author of the marvelous *Big Tiger and Christian,* knew some of this type of story, from his extensive travels in Mongolia and China. He later sent me the Muhlenweg version in a rough sketch; still later, he sent me the version printed in Walter Heissig's *Mongolische Volksmarchen,* published in Germany in 1963.

The Smart Shopper

I first heard this from a Romanian delegate to an IBBY Congress, whose name, sadly, I forgot to note. Some years later, I heard a very similar version from Angela Evdoxiadis of Toronto, whose parentage was Greek and Armenian. I subsequently discovered a similar version in Albania, when visiting schools and libraries with Mrs. Shpresa Vreto in 1994.

The Smart Shopper—Swiss and German Versions

This version is slightly adapted from one of two figures given in the delightful collection *Falten und Spielen,* compiled by Susanne-Stocklin Meier, one of a series of handbooks she compiled for parents and early childhood caregivers, on the importance of traditional play in the young child's life. I also came upon a version at the International Youth Library in Munich, Germany. Thanks to the late Elisabeth Waldman for pointing these out to me in 1980.

What Do You Think You Are?

A figure for this is given in *Falten und Spielen* (see previous entry) but no real story. I invented this version after a comment by a participant in a storytelling seminar at the International Youth Library in Munich, who told me it was a common trick to play on their younger siblings who were just learning to print the alphabet.

The Key

This is my adapted version of a story first told to me by Knud Eigil Hauberg-Tychsen at an IBBY Conference in Denmark in the 1970s. Per Gustavsson gives a somewhat different version in his book, *Ritsagor.*

Per's Trousers; Light Bulb

The first is from *Ritsagor* and the second from *Fler Ritsagor,* both by Per Gustavsson, and used with his permission. The translations are my own. I changed slightly the drawing in "Per's Trousers," making the homes of Per and his friend Lisa into pockets. In this way, the original sentences seemed to make more sense to me.

Katy Horning's version of the light bulb figure I heard during an evening of hilarity at the home of Ginny Moore Kruse in Madison, Wisconsin.

How to Get Rid of Mosquitos

I learned this from an oral telling by Irene Kulman Santa Cruz, a librarian and teacher from Fernando de la Mora, Paraguay. I adapted it slightly as I made my own translation.

Little Circle, Big Circle

At a workshop for the Kelompok Pencinta Bacaan Anak in Indonesia, I exchanged stories with a number of writers and storytellers. All of the participants seemed to know a version of this drawing story, but Mrs. Toety Maklis, one of Indonesia's best-known children's book writers, agreed to write it down for me, and to get a teacher to sing it on tape. This she did, and soon I was listening to Ika Sri Mustika singing it in Bahasa Indonesia and then in English. The Bahasa pronunciation is as follows: a = ah; e = uh; i = ee; u = oo; c = ch; s = ss as in "miss."

Lingkaran kecil, lingkaran kecil, lingkaran besar.

Lingkaran kecil, lingkaran kecil, lingkaran besar.

Diberi pisang, diberi pisang, diberi pisang.

Lingkaran kecil, lingkaran kecil, melingkar, lingkar.

Enam, enam; tiga bulut enam. Enam, enam, diberi sudut.

The notes for the verses are approximately as follows:

do re mi mi do, do re mi mi do, mi mi fa mi re

si do re re si, si do re re si, sol fa mi re do.

do re mi mi do, do re mi mi do, mi mi fa mi re

si do re re si, si do re re si, sol fa mi re do

do mi, do mi; do mi fa mi re do; si re, si re;sol fa mi re do

My version is only slightly changed from that version. I added an extra "big" to the third lines of the second and third verses, and in the third line of verse four, I added "up and around" to "coiling." In chanting this, I usually say, "six times six; that makes thirty-six," even though the original only implies it. This is so similar to Japanese *ekaki uta* that I feel sure it came from that country and was adapted to a Bahasa tune and words.

Good Night!; Right Answer, Wrong Answer

The Dewan Bahasa dan Pustaka, an institute in Kuala Lumpur charged with researching, publishing, and promoting the language and literature of Malaysian Bahasa (Malay), has been exploring for some years the means to keep this language rich and alive among the children and youth of Malaysia. They began experimenting with various means of incorporating storytelling into the curriculum. To this end, they held a workshop in Port Dickson, where I was invited to share what I could about storytelling in many parts of the world. During one session, I showed drawing stories from a number of cultures. At the end of that session, Ahmed Ghulam Jamaludin of Kota Baru, Kelantan, stepped forward. With a twinkle in his eye he presented these two stories, first in Bahasa Malaysia and then in rough English. Many of the other participants said they also knew the stories, but his versions were the most humorous. I have adapted them only slightly.

The *Doh* Bird

This was given to me by my longtime friend Bandana Sen, librarian at the American International School, New Delhi. She is Bengali, and a lively storyteller, having entertained and inspired a whole generation of primary school students there. The ending is my invention. She showed other stories based on Bengali letters, but they were not very translatable.

How Man and Woman Found Their Place in the World

This is loosely based on several of the clever picture stories found in Volume 1 of *Fun with Chinese Characters*. This series belongs in every library. It has very clear diagrams, enabling even the rank beginner to start drawing simple Chinese characters. Plus, it is tremendous fun to study the cartoonlike sequences and learn to appreciate a bit of Chinese humor.

I first picked up these volumes in Singapore in 1980 and have been using them ever since. The story has evolved over the years, and this version was perfected in the numerous schools I visited in Singapore during several visits for the purpose of attending the International Festival of Storytelling they have been holding each November.

The Absent-Minded Judge

On a visit to Korea in 1972, I spent time in the Folklore Collection at Seoul National University and learned about some of the types of storytelling common in Korea, past and present. Among the stories I was shown were drawing stories, many of them based on Chinese characters. The librarian there referred me to a booklet called *A Korean Night's Entertainment*, which I picked up and which includes a number of drawing stories. This is slightly adapted from a longer story in that collection. The other drawing stories are full of sexual innuendo, and I occasionally use them with adult audiences.

Ekaki Uta

All of the Japanese drawing stories given in this collection are based on translations made for me by Shigeo Watanabe and Sachiko Saionji Watanabe (no relation). Some of them use versions I gleaned while observing children doing drawing stories, notably on my visits to various schools and libraries, arranged by HOLP Publishers. These took place in all parts of Japan in 1974, 1979, and 1986, and I was accompanied by Sachiko and the late Mitsue Ishitake.

Shigeo helped me with translations for two to three versions of each story, found in Iwai, Kako, Koizumi, or Sugahara (see Bibliography). My versions combine information found in all the versions. Occasionally, I added a phrase or detail if it seemed to fit the original pun or idea behind the drawing.

For those wishing to sing or chant the refrains most commonly used with each picture sequence, I recommend getting a copy of the Iwai collection, which is filled with versions of the tunes. It is in Japanese, of course, but the melodies can be interpreted by anyone who reads music.

The Rainbow Snake

I first learned about sand storytelling from the late Jack Davis, who told me about many Australian Aborigine traditions of storytelling and to whom I owe the deepest debt of gratitude. I was so impressed with my first experience of such storytelling, I determined to use it in my sessions in the United States and other countries. Using some of the Walbiri figures from Nancy Munn's book (see Bibliography), I adapted them to a version of this story I had learned from Roland Robinson. Over the years I have simplified the drawings

SOURCES OF THE HANDKERCHIEF STORIES

Almost all of the figures in these stories I first learned from Cecile Beijk van Daal of Eindhoven, The Netherlands, and members of her family and friends, whom she asked to help me in my reconstruction of handkerchief stories. The stories are reconstructions of fragments pieced together from many informants who told me how their parents, grandparents, or other relatives used the figures in telling them stories. The exception is the figure and the story "The Peasant's Clever Daughter." I adapted this from a riddle story I used to tell during my New York Public Library storytelling days in the early 1960s. I have been unable to trace my original source, but I recall that it was a printed pamphlet in the research collection of the main library.

My thanks to Nancy Gloe, school librarian in Madison, Wisconsin, for pointing out the Halverson book to me. The description there, telling how a pioneer family used the babies in the cradle handkerchief figure to entertain a group of Native Americans helped me to expand the story into the version I give in this book.

BIBLIOGRAPHY FOR DRAWING STORIES

Ager, Lynn Price. "Storyknifing: An Alaskan Eskimo Girls" Game." *Journal of the Folklore Institute* (The Hague) 11, no. 3 (1975): 187–98.

Allen, Louise A. *Time Before Morning: Art and Myth of the Australian Aborigines*. New York: T. Y. Crowell, 1975.

An, Tzu-cheh. *Cracking the Chinese Puzzles*. Vol. 1. Hong Kong: Stockflows, 1982.

Berndt, Ronald M., and Catherine J. *The World of the First Australians*. Sydney: Ure Smith, 1965.

Coulmas, Florian. *The Writing Systems of the World*. Oxford: Blackwell, 1989.

Craddock, Ida C. "The Black Cat" and "The Wild Fowl." *Journal of American Folklore* (1987): 322–3.

Davis, Jack. "Story Traditions in Australian Aboriginal Cultures." In: *Through Folklore to Literature*, edited by Maurice Saxby. Sydney: IBBY Australia (1979): 133–50.

DeFrancis, John. *Visible Speech: The Diverse Oneness of Writing Systems*. Honolulu: University of Hawaii Press, 1989.

Dinesen, Isak. *Out of Africa*. New York, Random House, 1938.

Druce, Arden. *Chalk Talk Stories*. Metuchen, N.J.: Scarecrow Press, 1993.

Early, Maud G. "The Tale of the Wild Cat." *Journal of American Folklore*, 1897, p. 80.

Elkin, Adolphus P. and Catherine J., and Ronald M. Berndt. *Art in Arnheim Land*. Chicago: University of Chicago Press, 1950.

Folk and Traditional Music of Asia for Children, Vol. 1 (LP disc and booklet). Tokyo: Asian Cultural Center for UNESCO, 1975.

Frikell, Wiljalba, et al. *Hanky Panky: A Book of Conjuring Tricks*, edited by W. H. Cremer. London: J. C. Hotten, 1872.

Fun with Chinese Characters: The Straits Times Collection. Cartoons by Tan Huay Peng. Singapore: Federal Publications, vol. 1, 1980; vol. 2, 1982.

Gustavsson, Per. *Ritsagor*. Illustrated by Boel Werner. Stockholm: Alfabeta, 1995.

———. *Fler Ritsagor*. Illustrated by Boel Werner. Stockholm: Alfabeta, 2000.

Heissig, Walter, ed. and trans. *Mongolische Volksmärchen*. Dusseldorf: E. Diedrichs, 1963.

Hoffmann, F. R. *Grundzüge einer Geschichte des Bilderräthsels*. Berlin: Rud. Hoffmann Verlag, 1869.

Iwai, Masahiro. *Warabeuta—Sono Densho to Sozo* (Nursery Rhymes—Tradition and Creation). Tokyo: Ongakunotomosha, 1987.

Koizumi, Fumio. *Kodomo no Asobi to Uta* (Children's Drawing Play). Tokyo: Soshisha, 1986.

The Korean Night's Entertainment (Comic Stories), edited by Tae-Hung Ha. Seoul: Yonsei University Press, 1970.

Malbunka, Mary. *When I Was Little, Like You*. Illustrated by the author. Crow's Nest, Australia: Allen and Unwin, 2003.

Mallett, Jerry J., and Marian R. Bartch. *Stories to Draw*. Hagerstown, Md.: Freline, 1982.

McDonald, Megan. *Tundra Mouse: A Storyknife Tale*. Illustrated by S. D. Schindler. New York: Orchard Books, 1997.

Munn, Nancy D. *Walbiri Iconography*. Ithaca, N.Y.: Cornell University Press, 1973.

Nakanishi, Akira. *Writing Systems of the World: Alphabets, Syllabaries, Pictograms*. Rutland, Vt.: C. E. Tuttle, 1990.

Oldfield, Margaret. *Tell and Draw Stories*. Minneapolis, Minn.: Creative Storytime Press, 1963.

———. *More Tell and Draw Stories*. Minneapolis, Minn.: Creative Storytime, 1969.

———. *Lots More Tell and Draw Stories*. Minneapolis, Minn.: Creative Storytime, 1973.

Oswalt, Wendell H., and Helen T. Oswalt. "Traditional Storyknife Tales of Yuk Girls." *Proceedings of the American Philosophical Society* 108, no. 4, (1964): 310–36.

Parker, K. Langloh. *Woggheeguy: Australian Aboriginal Legends*. Adelaide: F. W. Preece, 1930.

Pellowski, Anne. *The Story Vine*. New York: Macmillan, 1984.

———. *The World of Storytelling*. Expanded and revised ed. New York: H. W. Wilson, 1990.

Pflomm, Phyllis Noe. *Chalk in Hand: The Draw and Tell Book*. Metuchen, N.J.: Scarecrow Press, 1986.

Robinson, Roland. *Legend and Dreaming*. Sydney: Edwards and Shaw, 1952.

Stocklin-Meier, Susanne. *Falten und Spielen*. Photos by Niggi Brauning. Zürich: Orell Füssli Verlag, 1977.

———. *Komm Wir Spielen*. Photos by Niggi Brauning. Zürich: Orell Füssli Verlag, 1986.

———. *Kranksein und Spielen*. Photos by Andreas Wolfensberger. Zürich: Orell Füssli Verlag, 1982.

———. *Spielen und Sprechen*. Photos by Niggi Brauning. Zürich: Orell Füssli Verlag, 1975.

Sugahara, Michihiko. *Asobo: Ekaki Asobi* (Drawing Play). Tokyo: Iseisha, 1986.

Tillhagen, Carl-Herman. *Svenska Folkelekar och Dansar*. Stockholm: Bokverk, 1949.

Van der Leeden, J. C. "Thundering Gecko and Emu." In *Australian Aboriginal Mythology: Essays in Honour of W. E. H. Stanner*; edited by by L. R. Hiatt. Canberra: Australian Institute of Aboriginal Studies, 1975.

Visser-Bakker, Jant, and Anneke Buizer-Visser. *Fan Tryntsjemuoi en Duotsjemuoi*. Ljouwert (Leeuwarden): Koperative Utjowerij, 1978.

———. *Van Trientjemoei en Dientjemoei*. Translated from the Friesian into Dutch by Wieke Veenstra. Baarn: Free Spirit Productions, 1981.

Wallace, Phyl, and Noel Wallace. "Milpatjunanyi, the Story Game." In *Children of the Desert*. Melbourne: Thomas Nelson, 1968, 24–6.

Withers, Carl. *The Tale of a Black Cat*. Illustrated by Alan Cober. New York: Holt, Rinehart, 1966.

Yoshida, Teiichi. *Bo Ga Ippon Attatosa*. Illustrated by Yoshitaka Shinohara. Tokyo: Rakuda, 1992.

———. *Happa no Naka no Happappa*. Illustrated by Yoshitaka Shinohara. Tokyo: Rakuda, 1991.

————. *Tamago ga Hitotsu Odango Futatsu*. Illustrated by Yoshitaka Shinohara. Tokyo: Rakuda, 1993.

Zelinsky, Paul. *The Maid and the Mouse and the Odd-Shaped House*. New York: Dodd, Mead, 1981.

BIBLIOGRAPHY FOR HANDKERCHIEF STORIES

Beard, Daniel C. "What Can Be Made with a Handkerchief." In *St. Nicholas Magazine*, 9, pt. 2 (Oct. 1882): 972–6.

Braun-Ronsdorf, Margarete. *The History of the Handkerchief*. Leigh-on-Sea, England: F. Lewis, 1961.

Burns, Elizabeth. *Hanky Panky*. Aptos, Calif.: E. Burns, 1986.

Frikell, Wiljalba, et al. *Hanky Panky; a Book of Conjuring Tricks*, edited by W. H. Cremer. London: J. C. Hotten, 1872.

Gustafson, Helen. *Hanky Panky: An Intimate History of the Handkerchief*. Photos by Jonathan Chester. Berkeley, Calif.: Ten Speed Press, 2002

Jackson, Paul. *Hanky Panky; 17 Models to Make with the Handkerchief in Your Pocket*. North Ryde, NSW, Australia: Angus and Robertson, 1990.

Jacobs, Frances. *Out of a Handkerchief*. New York: Lothrop, 1942.

Leske, Marie. *Illustriertes Spielbuch für Mädchen*. Leipzig: Otto Spamer, 1871.

Pellowski, Anne. *The Family Storytelling Handbook*. New York: Macmillan, 1987.

Peters-Holger, Katherina. *Das Taschentuch; eine theatergeschichtliche Studie*. Emsdetten, Westfalen: Verlag Lechte, 1961.

Seymour, Alta Halverson. *Galewood Crossing*. Philadelphia: Westminster, 1946.

Taschentuch in Tracht und Brauch; Volkskunde, Fakten und Analysen. Wien: Verein für Volkskunde, 1972.

Vance, Eleanor Graham. *The Everything Book*. Illustrated by Trina S. Hyman. New York: Golden Press, 1974.

Index

About the Author

ANNE PELLOWSKI a former librarian from New York Public Library, and renowned storyteller and author, has published such titles as *The Story Vine*, *World of Children's Stories*, *Family Storytelling Handbook*, and others. She performs and conducts storytelling workshops around the world. Drawing stories are among those most requested by librarians and teachers.